Josiah Harmar Penniman

The War Of The Theatres

Josiah Harmar Penniman

The War Of The Theatres

ISBN/EAN: 9783337116347

Printed in Europe, USA, Canada, Australia, Japan

Cover: Foto ©Thomas Meinert / pixelio.de

More available books at www.hansebooks.com

Publications of the University of Pennsylvania

Series in
Philology Literature and Archæology

Vol. IV   No. 3

THE WAR OF THE THEATRES

BY

JOSIAH H. PENNIMAN

ASSISTANT PROFESSOR OF ENGLISH LITERATURE IN THE
UNIVERSITY OF PENNSYLVANIA

GINN & COMPANY   MAX NIEMEYER
Agents for United States, Canada and England   Agent for the Continent of Europe
9–13 Tremont Place, Boston, U.S.A.   Halle, a. S., Germany.

THE Papers of this Series, prepared by Professors and others connected with the University of Pennsylvania, will take the form of Monographs on the subjects of Philology, Literature, and Archæology, whereof about 200 or 250 pages will form a volume. Each Monograph, however, is complete in itself.

The price to subscribers to the Series will be $2.00 per volume; to others than subscribers the numbers will be sold separately at the regular prices.

It is the intention of the University to issue these Monographs from time to time as they shall be prepared.

Each author assumes the responsibility of his own contribution.

75390

PREFACE.

This monograph contains some results of the study of a group of Elizabethan plays, closely related to each other, because all connected with the quarrel of Jonson and Marston, an incident in the history of the drama to which has been given the name "The War of the Theatres." Single plays and the plays of individual authors have long occupied the attention of critics and editors, but the intimate relationship of groups of plays, as a feature of what we may term the organic unity of the Elizabethan drama, has received from students less attention than it deserves.

The purpose of the present treatment is to set forth some conclusions concerning the plays, and the facts upon which the conclusions are based. A number of erroneous views that have been held by critics are referred to incidentally, but it has been no part of the plan to discuss all of the numerous mistakes that have been made in attempts to identify characters.

I take pleasure in acknowledging here the courteous interest in this work which has been shown by Mr. F. G. Fleay of London, and also the kindness of my colleague Dr. Child, who made the index; but especially do I wish to record my grateful appreciation of the valuable suggestions and generous aid of my friend and teacher Professor Schelling.

JOSIAH H. PENNIMAN.

University of Pennsylvania,
May 24, 1897.

THE WAR OF THE THEATRES.

I.

THE SATIRES OF MARSTON.

"THE War of the Theatres" is a term which has been applied to the quarrels of Marston and Dekker with Ben Jonson, which found expression in satirical plays. To this "war" is due the close relationship which exists between the works of these dramatists between 1598 and 1602. Whether any other dramatists took part in this contest is almost wholly conjectural, and the present discussion of the subject will be confined chiefly to the works of the three authors mentioned. That Shakespeare may have taken a hand in the quarrel seems altogether likely from the well-known passage in *The Return from Parnassus;* but there is no other direct evidence that he did, and the indirect evidence is, unfortunately, inconclusive.

This monograph is an attempt to show the relationship of the plays of which it treats, as regards the personal satire contained in them, by setting forth such evidence as has been found for the identification of the characters. The plays which will be discussed, in whole or in part, are *Every Man in his Humour, Histriomastix, The Case is Altered, Every Man out of his Humour, Patient Grissil, Jack Drum, Cynthia's Revels, Antonio and Mellida,* Part I., *Poetaster, Satiromastix, What you Will, The Return from Parnassus,* and *Troilus and Cressida.*

"The War of the Theatres" has been commented upon by many critics at various times, and there exists almost unanimity of opinion that Marston's Satires were in some way the cause of the quarrel. There has been, however, a difference of opinion as to the passages in which Jonson is by some critics supposed to be satirized. Two passages in Marston's *Scourge of Villanie* contain allusions to Torquatus, and it has been accepted traditionally that Jonson is the person intended. If this interpretation of the passages is correct, then *The Scourge of Villanie* (1598) is the earliest *extant* literary expression of the differences between Jonson and Marston. Against the theory that *The Scourge of Villanie* is the first attack on Jonson, must be taken into consideration his own statements concerning the beginning of the quarrel. In the *Apologetical Dialogue* appended to *Poetaster*, first printed in the folio of 1616, and stated to have been "only once spoken upon the stage," Jonson says:—

>   but sure I am, three years
> They did provoke me with their petulant styles
> On every stage; and I at last, unwilling,
> But weary, I confess, of so much trouble,
> Thought I would try if shame could win upon 'em.[1]

This is Jonson's first direct mention of the subject. His second direct mention of the "War of the Theatres" is in the *Conversations with Drummond*.

He had many quarrels with Marston, beat him, and took his pistol from him, wrote his *Poetaster* on him; the beginning of them were that Marston represented him in the stage, in his youth given to venerie.[2]

---

[1] *Works of Ben Jonson*, ed. 1640, I. 308.
[2] *Notes of Ben Jonson's Conversations with William Drummond of Hawthornden*, edited by David Laing, Shakespeare Society, London, 1842, p. 20.

Both these statements attribute the beginning of the quarrel to some *stage* representation, which, of course, could not apply to *The Scourge of Villanie*, a satire in verse.

Out of respect to tradition, and despite the statement just made, we must examine Marston's Satires. The critics have in almost every case dismissed the matter with a simple affirmation, and in no instance has any good reason for the identification of Torquatus with Jonson been vouchsafed. It is often extremely difficult at this late date fully to understand a meaning which may have been clear to Elizabethan readers, and many allusions must forever remain wholly unrecognized as such. A careful examination of the allusions of Marston to Torquatus is productive of some interesting evidence that the traditional identification of Torquatus with Jonson is correct. While it is undoubtedly true that much of Marston's satire is aimed at his rival Hall,[1] yet the allusions to Torquatus seem to be somewhat distinct from the general satire.

The first mention of Torquatus is in a note prefixed to the first edition of *The Scourge of Villanie*, 1598. It is as follows :—

TO THOSE THAT SEEME JUDICIALL PERUSERS.

Knowe, I hate to affect too much obscuritie and harshnesse, because they profit no sense. To note vices, so that no man can understand them, is as fond as the French execution in picture. Yet there are some (too many) that thinke nothing good that is so curteous as to come within their reach. Tearming all Satyres bastard which are not palpable darke, and so rough writ that the hearing of them read would set a mans teeth on edge ; for whose unseasoned palate I wrote the first Satyre, in some places too obscure, in all places mislyking me. Yet when by some scurvie chaunce it shall come into the late perfumed fist of judiciall Torquatus (that like some rotten stick in a troubled water, hath gotte a great deale of barmie froth to

---

[1] For a discussion of this point, see *The Works of John Marston*, edited by A. H. Bullen, 1887, I. xvii-xxiv.

stick to his sides), I knowe hee will vouchsafe it some of his new-minted epithets (as reall, intrinsecate, Delphicke),[1] when in my conscience hee understands not the least part of it. But from thence proceedes his judgment. Persius is crabby,[2] because auntient, and his jerkes (being perticulerly given to private customes of his time) dusky. Juvenall (upon the like occasion) seemes to our judgment, gloomy, etc.

W. KINSAYDER.

The three editors of Marston, Halliwell,[3] Dr. Grosart,[4] and Mr. Bullen,[5] make the following comments on Torquatus and the "new-minted epithets."

Halliwell, in his Preface,[6] speaking of the quarrel between Marston and Jonson, does nothing more than quote approvingly Gifford's note on *Poetaster*, V. 1, in which, after speaking of the terms used by Marston and ridiculed by Jonson, Gifford says:—

The works which our author had chiefly in view [*i.e.* in *Poetaster*] were *The Scourge of Villanie* and the two parts of *Antonio and Mellida*. In the former of these, Jonson is ridiculed under the name of Torquatus, for his affected use of "new-minted words," such as *reall, intrinsecate,* and *Delphicke,* which are all found in his earliest comedies.[7]

Dr. Grosart in the Preface to his edition of *Marston's Poems* thus comments on the Satires:—

I do not know the "venerie" allusions in Marston's play, or plays, that aroused the anger of Jonson. But "browne Ruscus" of the opening of

---

[1] Rev. Thomas Corser says that *Torquatus . . . reall, intrinsecate, Dephicke,* refers to Hall. *Collectanea Anglo-Poetica,* V. 13.

[2] Hall calls Persius "crabbed," Horace, "more smooth." *Virgidemiarum,* Book V. Sat. I. line 10.

[3] *The Works of John Marston,* reprinted from the original editions, with notes and some account of his Life and Writings, by J. O. Halliwell, London, 1856.

[4] *John Marston's Poems,* edited by A. B. Grosart, Manchester, 1879.

[5] *The Works of John Marston,* ed. Bullen, Boston, 1887.

[6] p. xii.

[7] *The Works of Ben Jonson,* edited by W. Gifford, London, 1816, II. 517.

Satire I. ... along with the *Metamorphosis* ... is a flagellation of him that must have told on the " Autocrat ... of the Mermaid." Torquatus, also of these Satires, unmistakably points to Jonson. Let the reader study *To those that seem Judiciall Perusers.* The words *reall, intrinsecate, Delphicke* are well-known Jonsonese.[1]

This, it will be seen, dismisses the whole matter without a particle of proof that Torquatus is Jonson, and the remark that "the words *reall, intrinsecate,* and *Delphicke* are well-known Jonsonese" is rather bold when we find by careful examination of Jonson's works only six instances in which any one of these three words is used.[2]

Mr. Bullen, the most recent editor of Marston, calls the allusion to Torquatus and the "new-minted epithets" "a hit at Ben Jonson,"[3] and in his Introduction thus comments on the passage : —

> In the address " To those that seem Judiciall Perusers " prefixed to *The Scourge of Villanie*, Marston undoubtedly ridicules Ben Jonson for his use of " new-minted epithets (as *reall, intrinsecate, Delphicke*)." *Reall* occurs in *Every Man out of his Humour*, II. 1: *intrinsecate* in *Cynthia's Revels*, V. 2, and *Delphicke* in an early poem of Jonson's. But as *Every Man out of his Humour* was first produced at Christmas, 1599, and *Cynthia's Revels* in 1600, these "new-minted epithets" must have been used by Jonson in some early plays that have perished.[4]

Mr. Bullen, it will be observed, gives not a single valid reason for supposing that Marston's mention of Torquatus in 1598 is an allusion to Jonson.

We must notice here the passages in the *Chronicle of the English Drama*, by Mr. Fleay, in which mention is made of

---

[1] *John Marston's Poems,* ed. Grosart, Preface, p. xlviii.
[2] Dr. Grosart's note on the allusion to Torquatus in Satire XI. of *The Scourge of Villanie* is mentioned below.
[3] *The Works of John Marston,* ed. Bullen, III. 305, note.
[4] *ibid.,* I. xxx.

Marston's Satires and their connection with the "War of the Theatres." The passages are as follows:—

> It is clear that the beginning of the turmoil among the three theatrical houses arose from Marston's abuse of Jonson, and praise of Daniel in his Satires.[1]
>
> Marston's Satires are very important for dramatic history. They were indirectly the origin of the three years' stage war between Jonson and Marston, Dekker, etc.[2]

A little further on we find:—

> But in all these Satires I find no one attacked but rival satirists, and no trace of enmity to Jonson or any playwright.[3]

The last passage seems to contradict the other two, which contain the correct view of the matter.

Let us examine the passages in Marston's *Scourge of Villanie* and see first whether there is any significance in the name Torquatus as applied to Jonson. We read in Roman History that Titus Manlius was called "Torquatus" because he slew a Gaul in single combat and took from him his *torques*, or chain, and wore it.[4] This stripping of the fallen foe constituted *spolia opima*. "Torquatus" as an adjective was applied to soldiers who were for special bravery presented with a *torques*, or neck chain. It was used also of anything which one might have around the neck. "Torquatus" as a noun might be translated "the man with something around his neck." With these facts let us compare certain facts in the life of Ben Jonson. In the *Conversations with Drummond* we find the following interesting parallel to the case of Titus Manlius. Jonson is quoted as

---

[1] *A Biographical Chronicle of the English Drama*, by F. G. Fleay, London, 1891, I. 97.
[2] *ibid.*, II. 69.
[3] *ibid.*
[4] *Cic. Fin.*, I. 7. 23.

having said that "in his service in the Low Countries he had in the face of both the campes killed ane enemie and taken *opima spolia* from him."¹

This is parallel to the deed for which Titus Manlius received his name "Torquatus." The second use of the term Torquatus, "the man with something around his neck," is not without a satirical application to Jonson, who is made to say that after his return from the Low Countries "being appealed to the fields, he had killed his adversarie, which [who] had hurt him in the arme, and whose sword was ten inches longer than his; for the which he was emprissoned, and almost at the gallowes."²

The original indictment shows that the duel was fought on Sept. 22, 1598, and that Jonson's arraignment at the Old Bailey was in October following. This document tells us with reference to Jonson's trial:—

> Cogn' indictament petit librum legit ut Cl'icus sign' cum l'r'a T, Et delr juxta formam statut', etc.

In English, thus:—

> He confesses the indictment, asks for the book, reads like a clerk, is marked with the letter T, and is delivered according to the statute, etc.³

Jonson escaped the gallows by his ability to "con his neck-verse." The adjective "Torquatus" has a peculiar significance in such a case.

Marston was a university man, having been given his B.A. by Oxford,⁴ and familiar with Roman history and the classic

---

¹ *Jonson's Conversations with Drummond*, p. 18.
² *ibid.*, p. 19.
³ The whole document is reprinted in *The Athenæum*, March 6, 1886, p. 337.
⁴ Halliwell says Marston got his degree in February, 1592, old style, *Marston*, I. v.; Mr. Fleay puts the date 1593, new style, *Chronicle of the English Drama*, II. 68; Mr. Bullen gives the date 1593-94, *Works of Marston*, I. xii.

use of the adjective "Torquatus." Moreover, as Jonson was a pedantic Latin scholar, a reference to him as "Torquatus" was a satirical compliment to his learning.[1]

The "late-perfumed fist of Judiciall Torquatus" may possibly be an allusion to the fact that Jonson had, as a consequence of his duel, been branded on the thumb with the Tyburn mark, as we are told in the passage quoted above from the indictment.[2]

Marston's *Scourge of Villanie* was entered, Stationers' Register Sept. 8, 1598, but it was probably not published until some weeks, or even months, after entry, and the fact that the duel occurred Sept. 22, two weeks after the date of entry recorded for *The Scourge*, does not seriously interfere with the probability of the allusion to Jonson's duel. The preface "To those that Seeme Judiciall Perusers" was, of course, the last thing written for the book, and touched upon an event which had just occurred. In the first passage in which Torquatus is mentioned,[3] he is spoken of as likely to apply to Marston's work "new-minted epithets," such as *reall, intrinsecate, Delphicke*.

Gifford affirms that these words are all "to be found in Jonson's earliest comedies," which may be perfectly true, but is no proof of the intended allusion to Jonson, because Marston's *Scourge of Villanie*, in which this allusion occurs,

---

[1] It is not impossible that the idea of stripping a fallen foe, connoted by the term *Torquatus*, from its application to Titus Manlius, may, when the same term is used of Jonson, contain an allusion to the incident related by Jonson to Drummond, "He beat Marston and took his pistoll from him." *Conversations of Jonson with Drummond*, p. 11. See also p. 20.

[2] There have been doubts expressed as to whether or not Jonson was actually branded with a hot iron, there being apparently no allusion to it in *Satiromastix*, in which almost every other incident in connection with the duel is mentioned. For a discussion of this point, see *The Athenæum*, March 6, 1886, p. 337, and June 19, 1886, p. 823.

[3] "To those that Seeme Judiciall Perusers."

was published in 1598, in which year *Every Man in his Humour* is the only extant work of Jonson's that had been acted. It is not necessary, however, that the words ridiculed should have been used in plays, as there is no particular allusion to Torquatus as a dramatist. An examination of Jonson's work reveals some interesting facts concerning his use of two of the ridiculed words in very early extant work. While it is well recognized that much of Jonson's earliest work has probably been lost, yet we have no right in the present case to base any hypothesis on non-extant work. Mr. Bullen seems to do this in his note quoted above.

Gifford noticed Jonson's use of the word *reall* (= regal) in *Every Man out of his Humour*, and remarked that in the quarto it is printed with a capital, " Real Entertainment."[1] In the quarto, 1601, of *Every Man in his Humour*, we find "and entertaine a perfect reall substance,"[2] and in the next scene we find Lorenzo, Junior, speaking of "reall ornaments." These uses of the word are probably prior to Marston's supposed allusion, for the quarto contains the text of the play as first acted and differs in many ways from the altered version of the play printed for the first time in the folio of 1616. The text as given in the quarto is the one to which Marston would refer in *The Scourge* in 1598.

Jonson uses *intrinsecate*, the second of the ridiculed terms, but not in any extant work earlier than *Cynthia's Revels* (1600), V. 2, a fact noted also by Mr. Bullen.[3] The third word, *Delphicke*, is found in Jonson's work and in two passages both very early. "Delphic riddling" is Jonson's translation of

---

[1] II. 1. [2] I. 1.

[3] "*Intrinsecate* is one of the 'new-minted epithets' that Marston accuses Ben Jonson, 'Judiciall Torquatus' of vouchsafing to his (Marston's) Satires. But 'intrinsecate' used also by Shakespeare, was at least sixty-eight years old when Marston wrote, for it occurs in the probably unique *Fantasy of the passion of ye fox lately of the towne of Myre a lytele besyde Shaftsburye in the dyouses of Salysbury*.

sortilegis Delphis in the *Ars Poetica*, line 219. As to the date of this we have Jonson's general, and probably only approximately correct, statement in 1619, that this translation of the *Ars Poetica* was made " twenty years since." [1] Accepting this as an exact statement, the date would be 1599 ; but there is no reason why it might not have been 1598 or even earlier, as the expression " twenty years since " may certainly be taken as only approximate. The fact that Jonson "keept [it] long in wrytt as a secret " [2] may indicate that Marston could not have seen it as early as 1598.

One other use of the word *Delphic* occurs in the *Ode to Desmond, Underwoods*, XLIII. We have no evidence that Marston ever saw these passages, but it is significant that they exist at all in early work. A much later use of the word by Jonson is to be found in his *Timber* in the *Character principis*, where he speaks of the " Delphic sword." [3]

These uses of the terms ridiculed by Marston are not in themselves conclusive proof that Jonson was meant by Torquatus, but they may fairly be said to show (1) that these three unusual words do find a place in Jonson's vocabulary ; (2) that they are all in early work ; (3) that one word, *real*, is used in work probably earlier than Marston's ridicule in 1598 ; another

---

Imprinted by me Wynkyn de Worde ye xvi day of February. The yere of our Lorde MVCXXX, just printed by Mr. Henry Huth in the first series of his most rare *Fugitive Tracts:* —

' The dolour *intrynsecate* vext me ones or twyse
So sore that my wyttes were brought to confusyon.'"

F. J. F. in *Notes and Queries*, Series 5, Vol. III. p. 346.

[1] *Jonson's Conversations with Drummond*, p. 29.
[2] *ibid.*
[3] In this use of the word Jonson is translating the classic μάχαιρα Δελφική, and there is, therefore, nothing peculiar in his use of the word *Delphic*. This was suggested to me by my colleague Prof. W. A Lamberton. See also the note on this in *Jonson's Timber*, edited by Prof. F. E. Schelling, note, p. 42, l. 18.

word, *Delphicke*, is used in work possibly earlier than the ridicule.

These various tests of the applicability of the allusion to Torquatus and his "new-minted epithets" to Jonson are cumulative, and make it all but certain that he was the man intended.

In every attack made by Jonson upon Marston we find Marston's vocabulary made an object of ridicule, the most direct and severe attack being in *Poetaster*, Act V. Sc. 1, where Crispinus is made to disgorge words used by Marston. This fact tends to establish yet more firmly the conclusion that it is Jonson whose "new-minted epithets" are attacked in *The Scourge of Villanie*.

It remains to notice the second allusion to Torquatus in Satire XI. of *The Scourge of Villanie*. The lines are —

> Come aloft, Jack, room for a vaulting skip,
> Room for Torquatus, that ne'er oped his lip
> But in prate of *pommado reversa*,
> Of the nimbling, tumbling Angelica,
> Now on my soule his very intellect
> Is nought but a curvetting sommerset.[1]

Dr. Grosart is the only editor that has offered any suggestion as to the meaning of this allusion, his remark being, "I cannot speak certainly whether 'Sommerset' be meant for a hidden stroke at 'Torquatus,' *i.e.* Jonson's adulation of 'Somerset.'"[2]

Mr. Bullen's only comment on this passage is, "The *pommado* was the vaulting on a horse (without touching the stirrups) and the *pommado reversa* was the vaulting off again."[3] Halliwell does not notice this passage at all.

---

[1] *The Scourge of Villanie*, Sat. XI. ll. 98-103.
[2] *Marston's Poems*, ed. Grosart, Introd., p. xlix.
[3] *The Works of Marston*, III. 375.

Other passages in Marston's Satires have been supposed to refer to Jonson. To these various identifications we can reply only that we do not know that they were not meant for Jonson; we have no proof that they were.[1]

---

[1] Dr. Grosart thinks that "browne Ruscus" (*Metamorphosis of Pigmalion's Image and Certaine Satyres*, Sat. I. 5–10) was meant for Jonson. *Marston's Poems*, Preface, p. xlviii. The lines are —

> Tell me, browne Ruscus, hast thou Gyges ring,
> That thou presum'st as if thou wert unseene?
> If not why in thy wits halfe capreall,
> Lett'st thou a superscribed letter fall?
> And from thyselfe unto thyselfe doost send,
> And in the same, thyselfe thyselfe commend?

In *Every Man out of his Humour*, l. 1, Carlo suggests to Sogliardo a device with a letter similar to the device mentioned above. Marston's lines were published in 1598, while Jonson's play was not performed until 1599, so that there can hardly be any allusion to it.

Tubrio, in the same work of Marston's, Sat. I. 89–125 and Sat. II. 118–119, has been by some thought to be an attack on Jonson's licentiousness, of which he told Drummond. (*Conversations*, p. 21.) The passage in Satire II. is —

> 'T is loose-legg'd Lais, that same common drab
> For whom good Tubrio took the mortal stab.

Mr. Bullen says (*Works of Marston*, III. 273), "It has been suggested without the slightest shadow of foundation, that the allusion is to the death of Marlowe." Dr. Nicholson says (in Grosart's *Marston*, p. xlvi, quoted by Mr. Bullen), "If Tubrio be Marlowe, then the hitherto unknown courtesan was the hermaphroditic 'Moll Cutpurse.'" Dr. Grosart says (*Marston*, p. xlvii), "If Marlowe be there pointed at, what possible ground can there be for separating the earlier description (*i.e.* Sat. I. 89–125) from the later?"

II.

EVERY MAN IN HIS HUMOUR.

The first play to be considered in our discussion of "The War of the Theatres" is Ben Jonson's comedy, *Every Man in his Humour*, a play which, although it contains no mention of Marston, was yet closely connected with the "War," on account of the violent attack on Daniel which it contains. The play shows plainly the arrogance of Ben Jonson's attitude toward his contemporaries; and the satire of Daniel, who was then popular and prominent, aroused opposition against the author of the attack. Why Jonson attacked Daniel, whom so many of his other contemporaries praised, we do not know; but it is altogether probable that Daniel's close connection with the court, shown by the tradition that he succeeded to the position held by Spenser, who was virtually poet laureate, made him the great obstacle in the way of Jonson, who was ambitious for court preferment. It was after this attack on Daniel that we find Jonson attacked by Marston in *The Scourge of Villanie*, and probably also in *Histriomastix*.

Every Man in his Humour has come down to us in two very different forms, an earlier, given in the quarto 1601, and a later, given in the folio 1616. The quarto gives the play as it was first performed, and is therefore the text with which we are chiefly concerned in the present discussion. The controversies concerning the date of the first production of the play do not especially concern us in the present connection, and it is enough for us to know that the play had certainly been performed in 1598, a fact of which Jonson informs us on the title-page in the folio of 1616.[1]

The Prologue to *Every Man in his Humour* is clearly an attack on methods employed by other playwrights, but all attempts to show that particular plays of Shakespeare, or any other dramatist, were aimed at, lose their force when we consider that criticisms on methods of dramatic construction were very common at the time. We find criticisms precisely similar to those of Jonson's Prologue in Whetstone's Dedication of *Promos and Cassandra*,[2] printed in 1578; in Sidney's *Apologie for Poetrie*,[3] written probably as early as 1581; also in *A Warn-*

---

[1] *Henslowe's Diary* contains records of the performance of a play called *The Comodey of Umers* on eleven dates between May 11 and Oct. 11, 1597. *Henslowe's Diary*, ed. J. P. Collier, Shakespeare Society, 1845, pp. 87–91. Some have thought that these entries refer to Jonson's *Every Man in his Humour*. Mr. Fleay says that *The Comodey of Umers* was "certainly the same play" as Chapman's *A Humorous Day's Mirth. Chronicle of the English Drama*, I. 55. Jonson was in the employ of Henslowe in 1597, as several entries in the *Diary* show. See *Henslowe's Diary*, pp. 255, 256. For a discussion of the date of first production of *Every Man in his Humour*, see Dr. Brinsley Nicholson's articles in *The Antiquary*, July, 1882, pp. 15–19 and September, 1882, pp. 106–110; also *Chronicle of the English Drama*, Fleay, I. 358. The quarto has the following title-page: *Every Man in his Humor | as it hath been sundry times | publickly acted by the right Honorable the Lord Cham | berlaine his servants. | Written by Ben Johnson. Quod non dant proceres, dabit Histrio | Haud tamen invidias vati, quem pulpita pascunt. | Imprinted at London, for Walter Burre, and are to | be sould at his shoppe in Paules church-yarde | 1601.*

The play in this earlier form differs considerably from the folio text of 1616. The characters in the quarto bear Italian names, of which the list is as follows (with the names as given by the folio, in parentheses): Lorenzo Senior (Knowell), Thorello (Kitely), Prospero (Wellbred), Stephano (Stephen), Doctor Clement (Justice Clement), Bobadilla (Bobadil), Musco (Brainworm), Giulliano (Downright), Lorenzo Junior (Edward Knowell), Biancha (Dame Kitely), Hesperida (Bridget), Peto (Formal), Matheo (Mathew), Pizo (Cash), Cob (Cob), Tib (Tib).

The two texts differ considerably, one of the chief instances being in Act V., in which a long speech of Lorenzo Junior in defence of poetry has been omitted from the lines of Edward Knowell. Gifford gives the omitted passage in his note.

[2] *Shakespeare's Library*, ed. Hazlitt, Pt. II. Vol. II. p. 204.

[3] Ed. Arber, p. 64.

ing for Fair Women, 1599.[1] Other examples might be mentioned. If we try to explain Jonson's criticisms as referring to Shakespeare, or any other dramatist, we must explain also the allusions in all similar criticisms. As Jonson's Prologue was printed for the first time in the folio in 1616, and as we do not know when it was written, though various guesses have been made, there is nothing, so far as chronology is concerned, to prevent our referring Jonson's strictures to any plays of Shakespeare's to which they may be applicable. The Prologue is —

> Though need make many poets, and some such
> As art and nature have not bettered much ;
> Yet ours for want hath not so loved the stage,
> As he dare serve the ill customs of the age,
> Or purchase your delight at such a rate,
> As, for it, he himself must justly hate :
> To make a child now swaddled, to proceed
> Man, and then shoot up, in one beard and weed,
> Past threescore years ; or with three rusty swords,
> And help of some few foot and half-foot words,
> Fight over York and Lancaster's long jars,
> And in the tyring house bring wounds to scars.
> He rather prays you will be pleased to see
> One such today as other plays should be ;
> Where neither chorus wafts you o'er the seas,
> Nor creaking throne comes down the boys to please :
> Nor nimble squib is seen to make afeard
> The gentlewomen ; no rolled bullet heard
> To say, it thunders ; nor tempestuous drum
> Rumbles, to tell you when the storm doth come ;
> But deeds, and language, such as men do use,
> And persons, such as comedy would choose,
> When she would shew an image of the times,
> And sport with human follies, not with crimes,
> Except we make them such, by loving still
> Our popular errors, when we know they're ill.

---

[1] *The School of Shakspere*, Simpson, II. 242, 243.

> I mean such errors as you'll all confess
> By laughing at them, they deserve no less ;
> Which, when you heartily do, there's hope left then,
> You, that have so graced monsters, may like men.

That some of these criticisms are applicable to plays of Shakespeare is evident ; that they are applicable to the plays of other men is equally evident, but is a fact ignored by those who believe that Jonson and Shakespeare quarrelled. The chorus that "wafts you o'er the seas" may refer to *Henry V.* or to *Winter's Tale*, but it may also refer to the chorus in *The Life and Death of Stukeley*, 1600, which bids the auditors "Embarked and victualled think him on the sea."[1] "York and Lancaster's long jars" may refer to *Henry VI.*, Parts I., II., and III., or to the several old plays, upon which these plays were modelled. "The creaking throne" was a common device used in many plays, as in *Sir Clyomon and Clamydes*, 1599, in which Providence is "let down,"[2] or in *A Looking Glass for London and England*, 1594, in which Oseas is let down from the flies.[3] Violation of the unity of time is severely ridiculed by Sidney and Whetstone in the passages already referred to, and while it is possible to apply Jonson's line about "a child new swaddled," to *Winter's Tale*, it is equally applicable to numerous other plays, such as *Patient Grissil*, by Dekker. "The rolled bullet ... to say it thunders" and "the tempestuous drum" may refer to the opening scenes of *Macbeth* and *The Tempest*, or to *King Lear*, or to many other plays by other dramatists, in which storms are represented, as, for example, *Faustus*, *Locrine* or *Mucedorus*. One of the most absurd attempts to prove that Shakespeare was attacked in this Prologue is based on the fact that it was published in the year of Shakespeare's death.[4]

---

[1] *The School of Shakspere*, Simpson, I. 248.
[2] *Peele*, ed. Dyce, p. 520.   [3] *Greene*, ed. Grosart, XIV. 14.
[4] *Ben Jonson und seine Schule*. Wolf Graf von Baudissin, I. ix. See also *Essay on the Life and Dramatic Writings of Ben Jonson*, by Alexander Schmidt, Dantzig, 1847.

Whatever may be the allusions to particular plays there is no doubt as to Jonson's views of the function of dramatic representation as expressed in this Prologue. His play observes the unities, and holds up to view "popular errors." The characters are not merely types of classes, but in many instances undoubtedly represent individuals who were at the time living in London. Various guesses have been made as to the identity of the persons thus represented, and in many instances these guesses have been almost wholly unsupported by evidence.

It is apart from the purpose of the present discussion to mention all of the supposed identifications that have been made of the characters in the plays of which it treats. One or two guesses may be mentioned here, however, as showing the eagerness of some critics to involve Shakespeare in "The War of the Theatres."

Dr. Robert Cartwright stated in his monograph that in *Every Man in his Humour* Shakespeare was meant by Master Stephen, the country gull, and also by Wellbred.[1] The only reason given for the first identification is that Shakespeare spent his boyhood in the country, while the second is supposed to be proved by the fact that Edward Knowell, assumed by Dr. Cartwright to be Jonson, is "almost grown to be the idolater of this young Wellbred."[2] If either of these identifications could be proved, we should have an interesting situation, a man acting in a play in which one of the other characters represented himself, for, as we know from the list of actors published in the folio, Shakespeare was one of the Chamberlain's men, who produced this play. We learn from the play a number of facts concerning Master Stephen, and it needs no argument to show that, whoever else Stephen may be, he is certainly not Shakespeare.

---

[1] *Shakespeare and Jonson, Dramatic versus Wit Combats, Auxiliary forces, Beaumont and Fletcher, Marston, Dekker, Chapman and Webster,* London, 1864, pp. 22, etc.
[2] *Every Man in his Humour,* I. 1.

In I. 1, we are told that Master Stephen is "a country gull," nephew of Knowell; is interested in hawking and hunting; wants to imitate courtiers; dwells at Hogsden. He is called by his uncle "a prodigal absurd coxcomb." He wastes that which his friends have left him, and affects to make a blaze of gentry to the world. He is next heir to Knowell, if Edward Knowell die. He has a living of his own hard by. He swears all kinds of strange oaths. He is vain of his legs in silk hose (I. 2); is a coward and "protests." In II. 2, Master Stephen has a jet ring sent him by "Mistress Mary" with the "poesie":

> Though fancy sleep
> My love is deep.

to which he replies: —

> The deeper the sweeter
> I'll be judged by Saint Peter.

In the same scene Master Stephen buys Brainworm's rapier. In III. 2, Wellbred calls Master Stephen "a fool . . . it needs no affidavit to prove it."

Master Stephen's name is entered in the "Artillery Garden." In IV. 9, he wears Downright's coat and is arrested by Brainworm. Downright calls Master Stephen "Signior gull . . . turned filcher of late." Such are the facts stated concerning Master Stephen. When Master Mathew speaks of overflowing "half a score, or a dozen sonnets,"[1] Master Stephen replies "I love such things out of measure"; this, taken with the fact that he is friendly to Master Mathew, and praises the latter's poems, suggests the possibility that Master Stephen and Master Mathew in this play may be the same persons as Fungoso and Fastidious Brisk in *Every Man out of his Humour*, and Asotus and Hedon in *Cynthia's Revels*. It will be shown that Master Mathew, Fastidious Brisk, and Hedon are all represen-

---

[1] III. 1.

tations of Samuel Daniel, and that Asotus and Fungoso were meant for Thomas Lodge. In his desire to make a blaze of gentry, as well as in some other particulars, Master Stephen suggests Sogliardo in *Every Man out of his Humour.*

Another supposed identification, which has more apparent probability than the identification of Master Stephen with Shakespeare, is that of George Downright with Jonson. It is a well-known fact that Jonson does appear in each of his next three plays: as Asper in *Every Man out of his Humour*, as Crites in *Cynthia's Revels*, and as Horace in *Poetaster.*

Downright is "a plain squire," "half-brother of Wellbred." He brags that he will give Master Mathew the bastinado (I. 4). Bobadil threatens to beat Downright if he chance to meet him (I. 4), but is a coward when he does (IV. 5). Downright is "a tall, big man . . . he goes in a cloak most commonly of silk russet laid about with russet lace" (IV. 7). The general hostility of Downright to Master Mathew strongly suggests Jonson's hostility to Daniel, of which further mention will be made. Against any identification of Jonson in this play must be taken Dekker's statement made in his dedication of *Satiromastix* "To the world":—

I meete one, and he runnes full Butt at me with his Satires hornes, for that in untrussing Horace I did onely whip his fortunes, and condition of life, where the more noble Reprehension had bin of his mindes Deformitie, whose greatnes if his Criticall Lynx had with as narrow eyes, observ'd in himselfe, as it did little spots upon others, without all disputation, Horace would not have left Horace out of *Every Man in's Humour.*[1]

If any character in *Every Man in his Humour* had been a representation of Jonson himself, Dekker would not have omitted to mention the fact and the name of the character when he wrote in *Satiromastix:*—

---

[1] *Satiromastix*, Quarto, 1602, p. 3.

You must be call'd Asper and Criticus and Horace; thy tytle's longer areading than the stile a the big Turkes: Asper, Criticus,[1] Quintus Horatius Flaccus.[2]

Justice Clement is a clearly defined character. He lived on Coleman Street (III. 2); "he is a city magistrate, a justice here, an excellent good lawyer, and a great scholar, but the only mad merry old fellow in Europe. . . . He is a very strange presence, methinks; it shews as if he stood out of the rank from other men. I [Edward Knowell] have heard many of his jests in the University. They say he will commit a man for taking the wall of his horse . . . or wearing his cloak on one shoulder, or serving God, any thing indeed, if it come in the way of his humour" (III. 2); he will permit no one to speak against tobacco (III. 3); Clement always pardons culprits; will challenge the poet, Master Mathew, at *ex tempore;* he burns Mathew's poems (V. 1). It would seem that from these particulars it might be possible to identify the original of this character.

It has been thought by some that Clement may be Lyly.[3] Cob speaks of having been his neighbor eighteen years, which may possibly have reference to the date of publication of *Euphues and his England,* 1580. There are several points in which the facts concerning Lyly agree with what we are told of Justice Clement. Lyly graduated B.A. Oxford, 1573, and was granted the degree M.A. by Cambridge in 1579. He gained at Oxford the reputation of being "a noted wit." Nashe says that Lyly was an immoderate tobacco-smoker.[4] Joseph Hall, the satirist, when in charge of a parish at Halsted, in Suffolk, was opposed by a "Mr. Lilly," who has been

---

[1] Crites was called Criticus in the quarto of *Every Man out of his Humour.*
[2] *Satiromastix, Works of Thomas Dekker,* published by John Pearson, 1873, I. 200.
[3] *Shakespeare and Jonson, Dramatic versus Wit Combats,* p. 19.
[4] *Have with you to Saffron Walden. Works of Nashe,* ed. Grosart, III. 204.

thought to have been the author of *Euphues*, and who is described as "a witty and bold atheist." This was in 1601.[1] It is barely possible that Justice Clement's love of tobacco and committing a man for "serving God" may be allusions to the facts in Lyly's case. During the latter part of his life, and up to his death in 1606, Lyly lived in the parish of St. Bartholomew the Less in the ward of Farringdon without, and is buried in that church.[2] Justice Clement lived on Coleman Street, which was within "the city."

Kitely has been thought, absurdly, to be Ford, the dramatist,[3] but as Ford was not baptized until 1586,[4] it is impossible that he could have been represented by Jonson in 1598. Kitely is a merchant who took Thomas Cash "as a child" and christened him . . . and bred him at the Hospital" (II. 1). In V. 1, Kitely quotes a passage "out of a jealous man's part in a play."

> See what a drove of horns fly in the air,
> Winged with my cleansed and my credulous breath!
> Watch 'em suspicious eyes, watch where they fall.
> See, see! on heads, that think they have none at all!
> O what a plenteous world of this will come!
> When air rains horns all may be sure of some.

No editor of Jonson has discovered from what play these lines are taken. Kitely has not been identified.

Thomas Cash, whose name suggests Thomas Nashe, was servant to Kitely; bred at the Hospital (II. 1); "is no precisian nor rigid Roman Catholic"; "he'll play at fayles and tick-tack" (III. 2). The use of the exclamation "Martin!" (III. 2) suggests the Martin Marprelate controversy. Cash remains unidentified.

---

[1] *Dictionary of National Biography*, XXIV. 76, s. v. Joseph Hall. The Rev. Canon Perry, the author of the article, says of this "Mr. Lilly," "probably John Lilly or Lyly, author of *Euphues*." It is by no means certain that he was.
[2] *London Past and Present*, Wheatley and Cunningham, I. 117.
[3] *Shakespeare and Jonson, Dramatic versus Wit Combats*, p. 23.
[4] *Chronicle of the English Drama*, I. 230.

Brainworm claims that he has been in all the late wars, Bohemia, Hungary, Dalmatia, Poland; fourteen years a soldier by sea and land, shot twice at Aleppo, once at Vienna; has been at Marseilles, Naples, and Adriatic gulf;[1] slave in galleys thrice, shot in head and thighs (II. 2). In the same scene, in disguise, he sells his rapier. Some have thought[2] that the various battles and campaigns referred to are allusions to Jonson's own career. This can hardly be the case. Cob is descended from a herring (cob); is a water carrier (I. 3); is a cuckold (III. 2); is threatened with jail for speaking against Bobadil's tobacco (III. 3).

Bobadil is the braggart soldier who evidently appears a second time as Shift in *Every Man out of his Humour*, and a third time as Tucca in *Poetaster*. In his dedication "To the World," prefixed to *Satiromastix*, Dekker wonders "what language Tucca [and therefore probably Bobadil] would have spoke, if honest Capten Hannam had bin borne without a tongue. Ist not as lawfull then for mee to imitate Horace as Horace Hannam?"[3] Bobadil swears strange oaths; he was in the fight at Strigonium (III. 1); he has been to the Indies, where tobacco grows, and calls tobacco "divine tobacco" (quoting Spenser, *Faery Queen*, III. v, 32). He brags of having defeated several men at once, and proposes a plan by which twenty skillful swordsmen could kill forty thousand men (IV. 5).

Knowell "is a man of a thousand a year Middlesex land" (I. 1); says of himself, quoting in substance words of old Jeronimo in *The Spanish Tragedy*, —

---

[1] The quarto reads "America" for "Adriatic gulf."

[2] Gifford states in a note that "in the French version of this play we are told that this and what follows is an account of the campaigns really made by Jonson! It is a pity that the editors stopped here; a life of Jonson on the authority of quartermaster Brainworm would have been a great curiosity." *Works of Jonson*, ed. Gifford, I. 54.

[3] *Works of Dekker*, Pearson, I. 182.

> Myself was once a student, and indeed,
> Fed with the selfsame humour he is now,
> Dreaming on nought but idle poetry,
> That fruitless and unprofitable art,
> Good unto none, but least to the professors ;
> Which then, I thought the mistress of all knowledge ;
> But since, time and the truth have waked my judgment,
> And reason taught me better to distinguish
> The vain from the useful learnings.[1]

Knowell has been absurdly identified with Chapman, who could not well be represented as speaking the lines just quoted. Edward Knowell, who wished to be a poet against his father's wishes, is similar to Ovid Junior, in *Poetaster*, who wished to be a poet, instead of a lawyer, against the wishes of his father, Ovid Senior. Mr. C. H. Herford suggests[2] that the relations between Jonson and his step-father may have been shadowed in the pictures of the Knowells and the Ovids.

Edward Knowell is a scholar "of good account in both our Universities, either of which hath favored him with graces." He is almost "the idolater of this young Wellbred" (I. 1). He is of "fair disposition, excellent good parts," "a handsome young gentleman" (IV. 1). Knowell tells Edward Knowell not to write poetry, lest it be burned, as Mathew's was (V. 1). Neither Edward Knowell nor Ovid Junior, whom he so strongly resembles, has been identified. Lyly was favored with degrees by both Universities, but in no other respect does he resemble Edward Knowell.

Of Master Wellbred we know very little beyond the fact that his sister married Kitely, and that Downright accuses him of having "your poets and potlings, your soldados and foolados to follow you up and down the city." Wellbred answers

---

[1] *The Spanish Tragedy* V., Dodsley, V. 147.
[2] *Ben Jonson*, Mermaid edition, edited by Dr. Brinsley Nicholson, Introductory essay by C. H. Herford, p. x.

Downright's abuse by threatening to cut off his ears (IV. 1). Wellbred quotes Latin, " Quos aequus amavit Jupiter " (III. 1.), and is the intimate friend of Edward Knowell, to whom he sends the letter (I. 1).

The only character that has been positively identified is Master Mathew, who is a representation of Samuel Daniel. Jonson did not look with approval on Daniel's poetry, although Daniel was very popular with the public, and with such critics as Nashe, Spenser, and Lodge, all of whom, as well as Meres, had praised his poems.[1]

In his *Conversations* with Drummond, 1619, Jonson said several things about Daniel which show that the two men did not agree in their ideas of poetry. The following are the notes made by Drummond :—

> Said he had written a Discourse of Poesie both against Campion and Daniel, especially this last.[2] . . .
> Samuel Daniel was a good honest man, had no children ; but no poet.[3]
> Daniel was at jealousies with him.[4]
> Daniel wrott Civill Warres, and yett hath not one batle in all his book.[5]

While these statements were made in 1619 and give Jonson's opinion of Daniel at that time, yet they agree with the representations of Daniel in Jonson's early comedies.

---

[1] Nashe, in *Piers Pennilesse*, praised *Rosamond* ; *Nashe*, ed. Grosart, II. 60. Spenser, in *Colin Clout*, praised *Delia* : *Spenser*, ed. Grosart, IV. 50. In the Induction to *Phillis*, Lodge praised *Delia* ; *Phillis*, p. 6. Hunterian Club reprint. Meres praised *Delia* in *Palladis Tamia* : *English Poets and Poesy*, Haslewood, II. 150. There are many other passages in which Daniel was praised by his contemporaries.

[2] *Jonson's Conversations with Drummond*, p. 1.

[3] *ibid.*, p. 2.

[4] *ibid.*, p. 10. On this statement Laing has this note : " Jonson says (in a letter to the Countess of Rutland) that Daniel 'envied him though he bore no ill will on his part.'"

[5] *ibid.*, p. 16.

Master Mathew, the "town gull," is the person attacked most vigorously in the play.[1]

Cob says : —

You should have some now would take this Master Mathew to be a gentleman, at the least. His father's an honest man, a worshipful fishmonger, and so forth ; and now does he creep, and wriggle into acquaintance with all the brave gallants about the town, such as my guest is (O my guest is a fine man !) and they flout him invincibly. He useth every day to a merchant's house, where I serve water, one master Kitely's, in the old Jewry ; and here's the jest, he is in love with my master's sister, Mrs. Bridget, and calls her Mistress ; and there he will sit you a whole afternoon sometimes reading of these same abominable, vile (a pox on 'em ! I cannot abide them), rascally verses, poetrie, poetrie, and speaking of interludes ; 't will make a man burst to hear him, and the wenches, they do so jeer and ti-he at him.[2]

Master Mathew meets Bobadil I, 4. and quotes from *The Spanish Tragedy* (III) some lines which he praises. The lines are —

<blockquote>
O eyes, no eyes, but fountains fraught with tears !
O life, no life, but lively form of death !
O world, no world, but mass of public wrongs !
Confused and filled with murder and misdeeds !^[3]
</blockquote>

Bobadil also praises the lines and Mathew then recites lines which he says are "a toy of mine own in my nonage ; the infancy of my muses." The lines are as follows in the quarto :

---

[1] Master Mathew appears in ten of the twenty scenes into which the play is divided, as does also Master Stephen. Brainworm appears in eleven scenes, Bobadil in nine, Edward Knowell in eight, Kitely and Cob in seven each, Wellbred, Cash, and Knowell in six each, and the other characters in from two to five scenes each, Clement appearing in only two. In almost every scene in which Master Mathew appears he is held up to ridicule.

[2] I. 3. Folio text.

[3] I. 4. See *Every Man out of his Humour*, V. 1. where Macilente ridicules Sidney's sonnet, *Astrophel and Stella*, C, beginning "O tears, no tears, but raine from beautie's skies." Macilente quotes the expression "more than most fair" used in this sonnet.

> To thee, the purest object to my sense,
> The most refined essence Heaven covers,
> Send I these lines wherein I do commence
> The happy state of true deserving lovers.[1]
> If they prove rough, unpolished, harsh and rude,
> Haste made the waste; thus mildly I conclude.

Jonson here ridicules Daniel's love-poetry, for it will be shown that Master Mathew was meant for Daniel. Mathew and Downright could not agree, and the "hanger" that Mathew thought "most peremptory beautiful, and gentlemanlike" was pronounced by Downright "the most pied and ridiculous that ever he saw,"[2] a statement in which we have a criticism of Daniel's taste.

Daniel's language is evidently ridiculed by Mathew's expression, "un-in-one-breath-utterable skill."[3] One of the first direct attacks on Daniel is contained in the following passage:

Mat. Oh, its your only fine humour, sir; your true melancholy breeds your perfect fine wit, sir. I am melancholy myself, divers times, sir, and then do I no more but take pen and paper, presently, and overflow you half a score, or a dozen of sonnets at a sitting.
E. Know. Sure he utters them then by the gross. [*Aside.*
Step. Truly, sir, and I love such things out of measure.
E. Know. I' faith better than in measure, I'll undertake.
Mat. Why, I pray you, sir, make use of my study, it's at your service.
Step. I thank you, sir. I shall be bold, I warrant you; have you a stool there, to be melancholy upon?
Mat. That I have, sir, and some papers there of mine own doing, at idle hours, that you'll say there's some sparks of wit in 'em, when you see them.
Well. Would the sparks would kindle once, and become a fire amongst them! I might see self-love burnt for her heresy. [*Aside.*[4]

Mathew's poems are again ridiculed (IV. 1) in a passage in which he is charged with plagiarism:—

---

[1] The folio altered this to "turtle-billing lovers."
[2] I. 4. [3] I. 4. [4] III. 1.

Brid. Servant, in troth, you are too prodigal
   Of your wit's treasure, thus to pour it forth
   Upon so mean a subject as my worth.
Mat. You say well, mistress, and I mean as well.
Down. Hoy-day, here is stuff !
Well. O, now stand close ; pray heaven, she can get him to read ! he should do it of his own natural impudency.
Brid. Servant, what is this same, I pray you !
Mat. Marry, an elegy, an elegy, an odd toy —
Down. To mock an ape withal ! O, I could sew up his mouth now.
Dame K. Sister, I pray you, let's hear it.
Down. Are you rhime-given too?
Mat. Mistress, I'll read it, if you please.
Brid. Pray you do, servant.
Down. O, here's no foppery ! Death ! I can endure the stocks better. [*Exit.*
E. Know. What ails my brother? Can he not hold his water at reading of a ballad?
Well. O, no ; a rhime to him is worse than cheese, or a bagpipe ; but mark : you lose the protestation.

. . . .

Mat.   " Rare creature, let me speak without offence,
      Would God my rude words had the influence
      To rule thy thoughts, as thy fair looks do mine,
      Then shouldst thou be his prisoner, who is thine."
E. Know. This is in *Hero and Leander.*
Well. O, ay ; peace ! we shall have more of this.
Mat.   " Be not unkind and fair : misshapen stuff
      Is of behaviour boisterous and rough."
Well. How like you that sir ? [*Master Stephen shakes his head.*
E. Know. 'Slight, he shakes his head like a bottle, to feel an there be any brain in it.
Mat. But observe the catastrophe, now :
      " And I in duty will exceed all other,
      As you in beauty do excel Love's mother."
E. Know. Well, I'll have him free of the wit-brokers, for he utters nothing but stolen remnants.
Well. O, forgive it him.
E. Know. A filching rogue, hang him ! and from the dead ! its worse than sacrilege.

This is a severe criticism of Mathew's methods of writing poetry, especially as he is made to claim that he wrote the verses "*ex tempore*" that morning.

Hero and Leander, completed by Chapman, was first published in 1598, the year in which *Every Man in his Humour* was produced. Sestiads I. and II., the portion written by Marlowe, had been printed in 1593. Mathew has not quoted the lines correctly, but by this Jonson probably meant to indicate that Daniel, in making use of another man's work, did change it somewhat. Marlowe wrote : —

> Fair creature, let me speak without offence :
> I would my rude words had the influence
> To lead thy thoughts, as thy fair looks do mine !
> Then shouldst thou be his prisoner, who is thine.
> Be not unkind and fair : misshapen stuff
> Are of behaviour boisterous and rough.
> . . . .
> And I in duty will excel all other
> As thou in beauty dost exceed Love's mother.[1]

The chief attack on Daniel in this play remains to be noticed. It is in the last act, beginning in the folio with Clement's words : —

A poet ! I will challenge him myself presently at *ex tempore*.

The quarto text differs greatly from the folio in this act. The scene in the quarto is as follows : —

Musca. Marry, search his pocket sir, and thele shew you he is an author sir.

Clement. Dic mihi musa virum. Are you, are you an author sir, give me leave a little, come on sir, I'll make verses with you now in honor of the gods, and the goddesses for what you dare call *ex tempore ;* and now I beginne —

> "Mount the my Phlegon muse, and testifie,
> How Saturne sitting in an ebon cloud

---

[1] *Hero and Leander*, Sestiad I.

Disrobed his podex white as ivorie,
　　　And through the welkin thundered all aloud."
There 's for you sir.
Prospero. Oh, he writes not in that height of stile.
Clement. No; weele come a steppe or two lower then—
　　"From Catadupa and the bankes of Nile
　　　Where onely breedes your monstrous crocodile,
　　　Now are we purpos'd for to fetch our stile."
Prospero. Oh too farre fetcht for him still Maister Doctor.
Clement. I, say you so, lets entreat a sight of his vaine then.
Prospero. Signior, Maister Doctor desires to see a sight of your vaine, nay you must not denie him.
Clement. What! al this verse, body of me he carries a whole realme, a commonwealth of paper in his hose, lets see some of his subjects.
　　"Unto the boundlesse ocean of thy bewtie,
　　　Runnes this poore river, charg'd with streames of zeale,
　　　Returning thee the tribute of my dutie;
　　　Which here my love, my youth, my plaints reveale."
Good! is this your own invention?
Matheo. No sir, I translated that out of a booke called *Delia*.
Clement. Oh, but I wolde see some of your owne, some of your owne.
Matheo. Sir, heres the beginning of a sonnet I made to my mistresse.
Clement. That, that! who? to *Madonna Hesperida*, is she your mistresse?
Prospero. It pleaseth him to call her so, sir.
Clement. "In Sommer time when Phoebus golden rayes." You translated this too? did you not?
Prospero. No, this is invention, he found it in a ballad.[1]
Matheo. Fayth sir, I had most of the conceite of it out of a ballad indeede.
Clement. Conceite, fetch me a couple of torches, sirrha. I may see the conceite, quickly: its very darke!

　　The ridicule of Matheo consists chiefly in calling him a plagiarist. Daniel's Sonnet I. to Delia is in the quarto quoted correctly, and it is said to have been "translated . . . out of a booke called *Delia*." In the folio text Jonson does not mention the "booke called *Delia*" and has altered the lines to read thus:—

[1] Note the play on the meaning of the Latin *invenire*, to find.

> Unto the boundless ocean of thy face
> Runs this poor river, charged with streams of eyes.

At which Edward Knowell exclaims:—

A parody! a parody! with a kind of miraculous gift to make it absurder than it was.

Clement then burns the whole batch of Mathew's poems, and Knowell calls his son's attention to the fate of poets, whereupon Lorenzo Junior, in the quarto, utters his defence of poetry, from which Edward Knowell, in the folio, says that he has been "saved." The burning of Mathew's poems is the most important incident in the closing scene of the play, a fact which impresses the reader strongly with the idea that the play was especially aimed at the man who was represented in the character of Master Mathew. That Samuel Daniel was the man held up to ridicule there can be no doubt when we find his Sonnet I. to Delia quoted as being absurd. The fact that Mathew utters lines from other poets also affects in no way the certainty of the conclusion that he represented Daniel, for we are told several times that he was a plagiarist, and the author of *The Return from Parnassus*, 1601-2, while praising Daniel, joins to his praise a substantial repetition of Jonson's charge:

> Sweete hony dropping D:[1] doth wage
> Warre with the proudest big Italian,
> That melts his heart in sugred Sonnetting.
> Onely let him more sparingly make use,
> Of others wit, and use his owne the more:
> That well may scorne base imitation.[2]

---

[1] In the quarto, Daniel is spoken of by his initials only, in the passage in which the poets are "censured." The others, Constable Lodge and Watson, are mentioned by name. *The Return from Parnassus*, ed. Arber, p. 11.

[2] My colleague, Dr. Homer Smith, calls attention to the fact that, in the lyrical poems appended to the sonnets to Delia, XXXVIII., beginning "O happy golden age!" is little more than a translation of a chorus in Tasso's *Aminta*.

III.

HISTRIOMASTIX AND THE CASE IS ALTERED.

THE first attack on Marston by Jonson is found in *Every Man out of his Humour*. Two characters, Clove and Orange, are introduced for the sole purpose of "talking fustian" and of ridiculing certain unusual words used by Marston in *The Scourge of Villanie* and *Histriomastix* ;[1] the latter is mentioned by name,[2] and, as such mention amounts to ridicule, we are led to examine the play with care to see what there may be in it of a nature to anger Jonson.

Histriomastix, as we have it, seems to be based on an older play, the purpose of which was to show how the pursuit of learning was neglected by the people, who preferred other pleasures. The character in it who defends the pleasures of learning is Chrisoganus ; and in reading the play we find many things in which the scholar, Chrisoganus, resembles Ben Jonson. There is in the play a severe attack on some playwright in the person of Posthast.

There are two theories concerning the authorship of this play. The usually accepted theory, advanced and supported by Simpson, is thus stated : "The drama, as it has come to us, is manifestly the work of two hands and of two times. This is proved both by the confusion of the sub-play in Act II., and by the alternative endings of the play. As originally written,

---

[1] Under the general heading "Unknown Authors," Langbaine has this entry: "*Histriomastix, or The Player Whipt;* printed quarto, London 1610. This play was writ in the time of Queen Elizabeth tho' not printed till afterwards ; as appears by the last speech spoken by Peace to Astræa, under which name the Queen is shadowed." *An Account of the English Dramatick Poets*, 1691, p. 532.

[2] *Every Man out of his Humour*, III. 1. The passage is discussed below.

the sub-play was that of the *Prodigal Child*; as it stands now, we have both the original sub-play and another perfectly distinct one on *Troilus and Cressida* foisted in on its shoulders."[1] "The author of the new additions to the play is clearly Marston. His unmistakable swagger begins to appear in Act II., where he begins to transmute the academic philosopher, Chrisoganus, of the old play, into the poet-scholar Chrisoganus of the new."[2]

Simpson tries to show by a course of reasoning, the results of which do not concern us especially here, that the play in its original form was probably written by Peele at a date somewhere near 1590, and that "it was an academical exercise for young men at the universities or for schoolboys to act."[3]

The second theory concerning the authorship of *Histriomastix* is that of Mr. Fleay, who apparently considers Marston the sole author of the play in its original form and in the form in which we have it.[4]

The confusion between the characters Fourcher and Voucher (in IV. 1 and VI. 3) and the two endings of the play indicate alterations in the original form to adapt it for court performance.

It is perfectly clear that Ben Jonson was offended at the play, and that Marston is responsible for its extant form, containing, as it does, many words and phrases at which Jonson directed the shafts of his ridicule. Jonson's ridicule, in *Every Man out of his Humour*, of Marston's vocabulary used in *Histriomastix* and *The Scourge of Villanie* is the first direct reply to Marston's ridicule of Jonson's "new-minted epithets."

Jonson's attack on *Histriomastix* in *Every Man out of his Humour* in 1599 establishes an upper limit for the date of

---

[1] *The School of Shakspere*, II. 3.
[2] *ibid.*, p. 4.   [3] *ibid.*, pp. 9–14.
[4] *Chronicle of the English Drama*, II. 72.

Histriomastix. Since Marston is spoken of, Sept. 28, 1599, by Henslowe as "the new poete,"[1] the date of Marston's share in *Histriomastix* cannot be much earlier than that year. The date is probably 1599, before Jonson's play. "All the indications of date agree with this, and the year being thus settled, the fear of Spanish invasion ('the Spaniards are come,' V. 4) would seem to fix the very month of production, for it was in August that this dread was excited."[2]

Critics have been practically unanimous in the opinion that Jonson is represented by Chrisoganus, for the general character of the scholar-poet agrees closely with what we know of Jonson. That Marston intended the representation to be satirical is by no means certain, and Mr. Fleay may be correct in his opinion that Marston "meant to compliment Jonson, not to abuse him ; and the indirect compliment to the man who had been rejected by the strollers, and was now poet to the chief company in London, second only to Shakespeare, was as delicate as it was deserved."[3]

Chrisoganus is a scholar who cares not for the opinion of the multitude. He is also a poet, and on offering to write for the new company of players, Sir Oliver Owlet's men, is rejected,

---

[1] Lent unto W^m. Borne, the 28 of septembr 1599, to lend unto Mr. Maxton, the new poete (Mr. Mastone), in earneste of a Boocke called ——, the some of xxxx s. *Henslowe's Diary*, p. 156.

[2] The most interesting addition that Mr. Fleay has made to our knowledge of this play is the result of his argument as to the company by whom this play was performed at court. The alternative ending, in which Astræa personates the Queen enthroned, shows that the play was performed at court. Mr. Fleay says : "The only companies who performed at court in 1599-1600 were the Chamberlain's, the Admiral's, and Derby's. The plays by the Admiral's men were *Fortunatus* and *The Shoemaker's Holiday*. This one [*Histriomastix*] could not have been acted by the Chamberlain's men, as it is satirized by Jonson in a Chamberlain's play. It was therefore necessarily that acted by Derby's men, who at this time occupied the Curtain from which another company had been ousted and driven to travel." *Chronicle of the English Drama*, II. 70.

[3] *Chronicle of the English Drama*, II. 71.

and the position is given to Posthast.[1] Simpson thought that Posthast was Shakespeare, and Sir Oliver Owlet's men the Chamberlain's company.[2] An attempt has been made recently to prove Simpson's hypothesis.[3] If Posthast is Shakespeare, then it is impossible for Chrisoganus to be Jonson, for we should have Chrisoganus (Jonson) rejected as writer by Sir Oliver Owlet's men (the Chamberlain's company) at the very time that Jonson was actually writing for the Chamberlain's company, by whom his plays[4] which immediately preceded and followed *Histriomastix* were performed. If Posthast is Shakespeare, then Chrisoganus is probably Marston himself, an hypothesis for which there is evidence.

While the general attitude of Chrisoganus towards public opinion is similar to that of Jonson, there is no passage in the play which has been proved to be a definite and unmistakable allusion that will apply to Jonson and to no one else. There is no allusion to any of Jonson's works except the possible allusion to his translations and epigrams in a passage which is almost equally applicable to Marston. The passage is —

Chrisoganus. O did you but your own true glories know,
　　　　　　　Your judgments would not then decline so low !
Philarchus.   What ! Master Pedant, pray forbeare, forbeare.
Chrisoganus. Tis you my Lord that must forbeare to erre.
Philarchus.   Tis still safe erring with the multitude.
Chrisoganus. A wretched morall ; more than barbarous rude.
Mavortius.   How you translating-scholler ? You can make
　　　　　　　A stabbing Satir or an Epigram,
　　　　　　　And thinke you carry just Ramnusia's whippe,
　　　　　　　To lash the patient ; goe, get you clothes,
　　　　　　　Our free-borne blood such apprehension lothes.[5]

---

[1] *Histriomastix*, III.
[2] *The School of Shakspere*, II. 11 ; also p. 89.
[3] *The American Journal of Philology*, XVI. 3, article by Professor Henry Wood of Johns Hopkins University, *Shakespeare burlesqued by two Fellow Dramatists.*
[4] *Every Man in his Humour*, 1598, and *Every Man out of his Humour*, 1599.
[5] *Histriomastix*, II. ll. 57–67.

The tone of Chrisoganus' remarks is certainly that of Jonson, and the allusion to his poverty, "goe, get you clothes," is one of the regular forms of attack on Jonson. The "translating-scholler" who "can make a stabbing Satir, or an Epigram" may be Jonson, to whom the words are peculiarly applicable. In *Poetaster* (IV. 1) Demetrius (Dekker) mentions, as the chief offences of Horace (Jonson), "his arrogancy and his impudence in commending his own things" and "his translating." Jonson left numerous translations, and that he prided himself on them is shown by his mention of them in several passages[1] in the *Conversations with Drummond*, who says of Jonson, "but above all he excelleth in a translation."[2]

Marston seems to have no claim to the title "translating-scholler," but when we read the line, "And thinke you carry just Ramnusia's whippe," we are reminded of Marston's *Scourge of Villanie*, in which the first *Satire* boldly announces in its first line:—

> I bear the Scourge of just Ramnusia.[3]

This certainly seems to connect Chrisoganus with Marston. Apart from this, which may be merely a general reference to Chrisoganus as a satirist, everything points to Jonson rather than to Marston as the man represented. As Simpson remarks, Horace (Jonson) in *Poetaster* is expressly "made a satirist, and in the very title of *Satiromastix* is termed so, while in its scenes

---

[1] *Jonson's Conversations with Drummond*, pp. 2, 5, 6, 29.
[2] *ibid.*, p. 41.
[3] It is possible that this may refer to Jonson, although there is no passage in *Every Man in his Humour* to which it is an allusion. Dekker in *Satiromastix* (1601) makes Crispinus say of Horace, "he calles himselfe the whip of men," in allusion, probably, to the following lines in the Induction to *Every Man out of his Humour*:—

> I'll strip the ragged follies of the time
> Naked as at their birth—and with a whip of steel,
> Print wounding lashes in their iron ribs.

he flings about his epigrams."[1] If Chrisoganus is Jonson, Mr. Fleay's suggestion that the high-minded old scholar is a complimentary representation gains great weight from the following evidently sincere reply of Mavortius :—

Chrisoganus. Follow, and Ile instruct you what I can.
Mavortius. We followed beasts before, but now a man.[2]

A passage which is, with some show of reason, thought to refer to Jonson is the following, in which the players are bargaining with Chrisoganus for a play, with the result that he is rejected and Posthast retained as poet of the company :—

Belch. Chrisoganus, faith, what's the lowest price?
Chrisoganus. You know as well as I ; tenne pound a play.
Gulch. Our companie's hard of hearing of that side.
Chrisoganus. And will not this booke passe? alasse for pride !
I hope to see you starve and storme for books ;
And in the dearth of rich invention,
When sweet smooth lines are held for pretious,
Then will you fawne and crouch to Poesy.
Clout. Not while goosequillian Posthast holds his pen.
Gut. Will not our own stuffe serve the multitude?
Chrisoganus. Write on, crie on, yawle to the common sort
Of thick-skin'd auditours such rotten stuffs,
More fit to fill the paunch of Esquiline
Than feed the hearings of judiciall eares.
Yee shades, triumphe, while foggy Ignorance
Clouds bright Apollos beauty ! time will cleere
The misty dulnesse of Spectators eyes :
Then woeful hisses to your fopperies !
O age when every Scriveners boy shall dippe
Profaning quills into Thessaliaes spring ;
When every artist prentice that hath read
The pleasant pantry of conceipts shall dare
To write as confident as Hercules :
When every ballad-monger boldly writes

---

[1] *The School of Shakspere*, II. 4.
[2] *Histriomastix*, VI. ll. 138–9.

     And windy forth of bottle-ale doth fill
     Their purest organ of invention ——
     Yet all applauded and puft up with pride,
     Swell in conceit, and load the stage with stuff
     Rakt from the rotten imbers of stall jests ;
     Which basest lines best please the vulgar sense,
     Make truest rapture lose preheminence !
Belch.   The fellow doth talke like one that can talke.
Gut.   Is this the well-learn'd man Chrisoganus ?
     He beats the ayre the best that ere I heard.
Chrisoganus. Ye scrappes of wit, base Ecchoes to our voice,
     Take heed ye stumble not with stalking hie,
     Though fortune reels with strong prosperity.[1]

  The tone of this is undeniably that of Jonson. Simpson says : " A study of Henslowe's diary will show that before 1600 the highest price ever paid by him was eight pounds or nine pounds. The usual price varied from four pounds to six pounds. Jonson was the first to charge ten pounds. It was for *Richard Crookback*, about 1600." [2] This statement is not, however, accurate, for the date was not 1600, but 1602, and the ten pounds was not for a single play but for a new play and alterations to an old one. Henslowe's entry is —

 Lent unto bengemy Johnsone, at the apoyntment of E. Alleyn and Wm. Birde, the 24 of June 1602, in earneste of a boocke called Richard crockbacke, and for new adicyons for Jeronymo, the some of X li.[3]

  The speech of Chrisoganus, made as it is to Posthast and his players, and referring to the plays written by Posthast, is a distinct echo of Jonson's own accusations against Anthony Monday, as Antonio Balladino, in *The Case is Altered*, I. 1 (1598). Onion says of the well-known verse " My mind to me a kingdom is," "'T is somewhat stale," and Antonio replies,

---

[1] *Histriomastix*, III. ll. 179-215.
[2] *The School of Shakspere*, II. 6.
[3] *Henslowe's Diary*, p. 223.

"Such things are like bread, which, the staler it is, the more wholesome. . . . I do use as much stale stuff, though I say it myself, as any man does in that kind, I am sure. Did you see the last pageant I set forth?" Antonio will not write "new tricks" and "nothing but humours; indeed, this pleases the gentlemen, but the common sort they care not for 't; they know not what to make on 't; they look for good matter, they, and are not edified with such toys." "Tut, give me the penny, give me the penny, I care not for the gentlemen."

Chrisoganus tells Posthast to "Write on, crie on, yawle to the common sort of thick-skin'd auditours" and "load the stage with stuff rakt from the rotten imbers of stall jests: which basest lines best please the vulgar sense."

That Anthony Monday was satirized in Antonio Balladino is proved beyond the possibility of doubt by the fact that Antonio Balladino is " pageant poet to the city of Milan," and is "in print already for the best plotter." Anthony Monday was pageant poet to the city of London from 1605 to 1623, and, although the pageants from 1592 to 1604 are missing, it is the generally received opinion that Anthony Monday wrote them.[1] Meres, in *Palladis Tamia*, mentions "Anthony Mundye, our best plotter."[2] It is to this statement that Jonson refers in *The Case is Altered*.

Anthony Monday is probably the man represented in *Histriomastix* by Posthast, a character which agrees in so many particulars with Antonio Balladino in Jonson's play. Marston's

---

[1] *History of Lord Mayor's Pageants*, Fairholt, Percy Society, p. 32.

[2] *Palladis Tamia*, Haslewood; *English Poets and Poesy*, II. 154. Jonson's allusion to Meres shows that *The Case is Altered* is of date later than Sept. 7, 1598, at which time *Palladis Tamia* was entered S. R. Nashe, in *Lenten Stuffe* (*Nashe*, ed. Grosart, V. 299) entered S. R. Jan. 11, 1599, mentions "the merry cobler's cutte in that witty play of *The Case is Altered*." It is thus possible that *The Case is Altered* is the earliest extant play of Jonson, for it certainly antedates *Every Man out of his Humour* and possibly *Every Man in his Humour*, though the latter is not likely.

attack on Monday as Posthast will explain the hostility between Carlo (Marston) and Puntarvolo (Monday) in *Every Man out of his Humour*, which results in Puntarvolo's sealing up Carlo's mouth;[1] and that between Anaides (Marston) and Amorphus (Monday) in *Cynthia's Revels*.

In the Apologetical Dialogue appended to *Poetaster*, Jonson speaks of having been provoked by his enemies "with their petulant styles on every stage." If we take the word "styles" here as referring to manner of composition, we may suppose that the striking resemblance between the speech of Chrisoganus[2] and the opening speech of Macilente[3] is the result of an attempt, on the part of Jonson, to show Marston how that kind of a speech should be written. Both speeches begin with a line of Latin and continue with a comment on the sentiment expressed.

There remains to be noticed a piece of indirect evidence going to prove that Chrisoganus is Jonson. In the *Conversations with Drummond*, Jonson is reported to have said that —

He had many quarrels with Marston, beat him, and took his pistol from him, wrote his *Poetaster* on him: the beginning of them were, that Marston represented him in the Stage, in his youth given to venerie. He thought the use of a maide nothing in comparison to the wantoness of a wyfe and

---

[1] *Every Man out of his Humour*, V. 4.
[2] *Histriomastix*, IV. 1. 132.
   Chrisoganus (alone). *Summa petit livor, perflant altissima venti.*
      Then, poor Chrisoganus, who'll envy thee,
      Whose dusky fortunes hath no shining gloss
      That Envy's breath can blast? O I could curse
      This idiot world, this ill-nurst age of Peace, etc.
[3] *Every Man out of his Humour*, I. 1.
   Macilente (alone). *Viri est, fortunae caecitatem facile ferre.*
      'T is true: but Stoic, where in the vast world,
      Doth that man breathe, that can so much command
      His blood and his affection? Well I see
      I strive in vain to cure my wounded soul, etc.

would never have ane other mistress. He said two accidents strange befell him: one, that a man made his own wyfe to court him, whom he enjoyed two years ere he knew of it, and one day finding them by chance, was passingly delighted with it:[1]

Mr. Fleay is the only critic that has offered any explanation of the representation of Jonson by Marston as "given to venerie," and his explanation is that *Jack Drum* is the play, and Monsieur John fo de King the character representing Jonson.[2] The first of the "accidents strange" mentioned by Drummond corresponds almost exactly with an incident in the career of Monsieur John fo de King.[3] We are met with difficulties, however, if we consider this character to be the representation on the stage which was "the beginning" of the quarrels, for the play *Jack Drum* is admitted by all commentators to have been performed in 1600,[4] the year after Jonson's attack on Marston in *Every Man out of his Humour*. *Jack Drum*, therefore, cannot be "the beginning" of the quarrel, in spite of the apparent agreement with the statement made by Jonson to Drummond.

A very simple solution of the difficulty concerning Marston's representation of Jonson which was "the beginning" of the quarrel, is obtained by merely transposing two punctuation marks in the passage from Drummond quoted above. Place a period after "stage" and a comma after "venerie" and read the passage thus:—

> ... the beginning of them were that Marston represented him in the stage. In his youth, given to venerie, he thought the use of a maide nothing in comparison to the wantoness of a wyfe, etc.

---

[1] *Jonson's Conversations with Drummond*, p. 20. The passage is here given as printed by Laing.

[2] *Chronicle of the English Drama*, II. 74.

[3] *Jack Drum*, V. 1. 299 to end of Act.

[4] *The School of Shakspere*, Simpson, II. 127; *Chronicle of the English Drama*, Fleay, II. 72.

When once this change has been made, its necessity is so obvious that we are doing no violence to the passage in an attempt to prove a theory.[1]

Having shown that *Jack Drum*, while probably satirizing Jonson as Monsieur John fo de King, is too late to have been " the beginning " of the quarrel, we are forced to look for the first representation of Jonson by Marston " in the stage " in an earlier play, which can be no other than *Histriomastix*. The only character in *Histriomastix* that can be Jonson is Chrisoganus. There are so many indications of the correctness of this identification, that although no one thing proves it, yet the cumulative evidence may be accepted as conclusive.

The title of *Histriomastix* indicates that the object of the play was an attack on Posthast the poet. Allusion has been made to the two theories concerning the identity of Posthast, and some evidence has been adduced to prove that Anthony

---

[1] The passage with its new punctuation is similar in structure to other passages as recorded by Drummond, who frequently began a sentence with a participial construction. These are instances: —

" Being at the end of my Lord Salisburie's table with Inigo Jones, and demanded by my Lord, Why he was not glad? My Lord, said he, etc." *Jonson's Conversations with Drummond*, p. 22.

" Ben one day being at table with my Lady Rutland, her husband comming in, accused her that she keept table to poets, etc." *Ibid.*, p. 24.

It is entirely possible that a change in punctuation was made inadvertently by a copyist in transcribing the manuscript from which Laing printed Drummond's " notes," and when we consider that this manuscript was itself a transcript and not the original writing of Drummond, there seems every probability that the new punctuation suggested gives the meaning that Drummond intended. For an account of the way in which Drummond's notes have come down to us, see the Preface to Laing's edition, pp. 21-23.

Mr. Fleay quotes in two places (in his *Chronicle of the English Drama*, II. 71, 74) the passage from Drummond, the first time without comment, as if it were punctuated, as it has been suggested that it should be, with a period after " stage "; the second time, as punctuated by Laing.

Monday was the man attacked. Mr. Fleay gives further reasons for the identification of Posthast with Monday.[1]

The identification of Posthast with Shakespeare, proposed by Simpson, has been advocated recently by Professor Henry Wood of Johns Hopkins University, in an article to which reference has been made.[2] Only his conclusions need be mentioned here. Agreeing with Simpson, that Posthast is Shakespeare, and therefore "Sir Oliver Owlet's men" the Chamberlain's company, Professor Wood brings forward some interesting evidence to show that the plays of Posthast, the titles of which are *The Prodigal Child, The Lascivious Knight and Lady Nature, Troilus and Cressida*, and an unnamed play,[3] are burlesques of Shakespeare's *Henry IV., Sir John Falstaff and the Merry Wives of Windsor* (the original title), *Troilus and Cressida*, and *Henry V.* Resemblances, parodied lines, burlesqued alliterations are given to prove the hypothesis that Posthast is Shakespeare. We have already pointed out what seems to us an insuperable objection to any identification of Posthast and Sir Oliver Owlet's men with Shakespeare and the Chamberlain's

---

[1] "[Derby's men] at this time occupied the Curtain from which another company had been ousted and driven to travel. The shareholders among these latter, there is little doubt, were Kempe, Beeston, Duke, and Pallant, who had just left the Chamberlain's men, and this company is, I think, satirized in *Histriomastix*. The poet who accompanies them is a 'pageanter' (IV. 3); has been a ballad-writer (V. 2, VI. 5); ought to be employed in matter of state (II. 2); is great in plotting 'new' plays that are old ones (II. 2); and uses 'no new luxury or blandishment, but plenty of Old England's mother words.' He is certainly Anthony Monday. . . . .

"Posthast, like Monday, can sing *ex tempore* (II. 4); but his principal business is to refashion other men's plays, such as *The Prodigal Son* . . . and *Troilus and Cressida* (from Dekker and Chettle's play of 1599). The allusion 'when he shakes his furious spear' in this latter (II. 4) cannot, unfortunately, be fully explained, as the Dekker play is not extant; but it probably refers to something therein anent Shakespeare's drama on the subject in its earlier form." *Chronicle of the English Drama*, II. 70, 71. See also *History of the Stage*, pp. 137, 138, 158.

[2] See, above, p. 34, note.

[3] *Histriomastix*, II.

company. If Chrisoganus is Jonson, and it seems impossible to avoid the conclusion that he is, then Posthast is not Shakespeare, because Jonson was writing for the Chamberlain's men at the very time at which Chrisoganus was rejected by Posthast's company. Apart from this consideration there are other difficulties to be disposed of before we can believe that Posthast is Shakespeare. What we are told of Posthast agrees in almost no particulars with what we know of Shakespeare. We shall have to prove the identification on the principle *lucus a non lucendo*, or invent a new principle, that burlesque proceeds by contraries. Of course, the latter might, in exceptional instances, be the case, but only when there was special reason for such treatment of a subject or person. On this principle, then, we might explain the fact that Posthast is a "gentleman-scholar"[1] as referring to Shakespeare, who was neither the one nor the other. Posthast is carefully distinguished from the actors, whereas Shakespeare was an actor. While the evidence is, to say the least, unsatisfactory for any identification of Posthast with Shakespeare, the facts in the case apply almost without exception to the career of Anthony Monday. When Posthast sings *ex tempore* and Landulpho blushes at the "base trash" sung,[2] we are reminded that Anthony Monday was notorious for having sung *ex tempore* and having been hissed off the stage, facts which we learn from the author of *The True Reporte of the Death and Martyrdom of Thomas Campion*, 1581. What evidence has been found for the identification of Posthast is given by the critics referred to, Simpson, Mr. Fleay, and Professor Wood. We are especially concerned with *Histriomastix* only so far as it affects Jonson, and thus enters into "The War of the Theatres."

---

[1] *Histriomastix*, II. 1. 209.
[2] *ibid.*, II. ll. 304, 322.

IV.

EVERY MAN OUT OF HIS HUMOUR.

CARLO BUFFONE, a satirical representation of Marston in *Every Man out of his Humour*, is Jonson's reply to Marston's representation of him as Chrisoganus in *Histriomastix*. Jonson had, by his former plays, made enemies, against whom he wrote *Every Man out of his Humour*,[1] a play performed in 1599 by the Chamberlain's company at the Globe Theatre. Daniel, whom Jonson ridiculed as Master Mathew in *Every Man in his Humour*, appears again as Fastidious Brisk, but it is Marston, as Carlo Buffone, who now occupies the chief place in the satire by being the object of the most severe attack.

When the play was published Jonson prefixed to it a brief description of each character. Carlo Buffone is said to be —

> A public, scurrilous, and profane jester; that, more swift than Circe, with absurd similes, will transform any person into deformity. A good feast-hound or banquet-beagle, that will scent you out a supper some three miles off, and swear to his patrons, damn him! he came in oars, when he was but wafted over in a sculler. A slave that hath an extraordinary gift in pleasing his palate, and will swill up more sack at a sitting than would make all the guard a posset. His religion is railing, and his discourse ribaldry. They stand highest in his respect whom he studies most to reproach.

Jonson was so bent upon lashing Marston that, at the end of the Induction, Carlo is described by Cordatus as follows : —

---

[1] That the play provoked criticism by its personal satire is clearly indicated by this note in the quarto : —

"It was not neare his thought that hath published this, either to traduce the Authour: or to make vulgar and cheape, any the peculiar and sufficient deserts of the Actors: but rather (whereas many censures flutter'd about it) to give all leave, and leisure, to judge with distinction."

He is one, the author calls him Carlo Buffone, an impudent common jester, a violent railer, and an incomprehensible epicure : one whose company is desired of all men, but beloved of none ; he will sooner lose his soul than a jest, and profane even the most holy things, to excite laughter ; no honourable or reverend personage whatsoever can come within the reach of his eye, but is turned into all manner of variety, by his adulterate similes.

Jonson satirizes other persons, but he makes no other such violent and abusive attack as this on Marston. Carlo appears in the opening scene and gives advice to Sogliardo about becoming a gentleman. After a disparaging speech to Sogliardo about Macilente (Jonson), whom he had not observed before, Carlo turns to Macilente with " I am glad to see you so well returned, Signior," to which Macilente, who had heard what Carlo had said about him, replies, " You are ! gramercy good Janus." Carlo says of Macilente, " An you knew him as I do, you'd shun him as you would do the plague." Thus at the outset the antagonism and hostility between Carlo and Macilente are set forth prominently, and to Carlo's remark on leaving, Macilente says to himself : —

> Ay, when I cannot shun you, we will meet.
> 'Tis strange ! of all the creatures I have seen,
> I envy not this Buffone, for indeed
> Neither his fortunes nor his parts deserve it :
> But I do hate him as I hate the devil,
> Or that brass-visaged monster Barbarism.
> O, 'tis an open-throated, black-mouthed cur,
> That bites at all but eats on those that feed him,
> A slave, that to your face will, serpent-like,
> Creep on the ground, as he would eat the dust,
> And to your back will turn the tail and sting
> More deadly than a scorpion.

At the close of Act I. Cordatus says of Carlo that " he stood possest of no one eminent gift but a most fiend-like disposition, that would turn charity itself into hate, much more envy, for the present." The abuse of Carlo, that has been quoted, might be applied to others besides Marston, but when Puntarvolo addresses Carlo as "thou Grand Scourge, or Second Untruss of the Time" (II. 1) we have Marston pointed out beyond question [1] as appears from the following considerations: —

---

[1] Owing to mistaken ideas concerning Dekker's connection with "The War of the Theatres," Carlo Buffone has been thought by some critics to be Dekker. There are some conflicting statements on this subject in Mr. Fleay's *Chronicle of the English Drama*. Mr. Fleay says (I. 97): "I thought that, if anything was settled in criticism, it was the identity of Crispinus [*Poetaster*] and Carlo Buffone with Marston." This statement is correct, but in another passage (I. 360) we are told that "Carlo Buffone, 'the Grand Scourge or Second Untruss of the Time' is Dekker; Marston, author of *The Scourge of Villany*, being the first Untruss"; on page 363 it is stated that the characters in *Cynthia's Revels* are some of them repeated from those in *Every Man out of his Humour*, "Anaides (Dekker) from Buffone," but neither identification here is correct, for Anaides, like Buffone, is Marston, in spite of the statement on page 364, "The description of Anaides (II. 1) identifies him with Carlo Buffone (Dekker)." On page 368 Mr. Fleay says: "The description of Demetrius [*Poetaster*] as a rank slanderer, etc., is conclusive as to his identification with Buffone and Anaides." "Finally, note that Demetrius as much as Crispinus affected the title of Untrusser, neglect of which fact has led to the common mistake in making Marston Carlo Buffone" (p. 369). We find the statement made (II. 71) "Hence his [Jonson's] abuse of Marston; but not as Carlo Buffone, the Grand Scourge or Second Untruss of the Time (Hall being the first); for Carlo was Dekker." On page 75 "Anaides is acknowledged to be Marston" although in the statement quoted above it is said that "Anaides (Dekker)" is repeated from Buffone. In a letter to the writer Mr. Fleay says: "I changed my opinion about Buffone when I had written about half of it [*Chronicle of the English Drama*] and meant to correct the Dekker bits when revising for press, but the printer did not keep to the time promised in sending proofs and I had to correct many while in the country away from my bookshelves.... The statements I. 360, I. 363, II. 71 are certainly wrong; you are right, Carlo = Anaides = Marston = Second Untruss. The point I missed was that Dekker appears first in *Poetaster*. This belongs to you." Dekker was not attacked until Jonson knew that *Satiromastix* was being written and that Dekker had been "hired" to write it. Dekker has no claim to the title "Grand Scourge or Second Untruss of the Time," although he did, in 1601, "Untruss" the "Humorous Poet." Jonson had no quarrel with Dekker in 1599 when *Every Man out of his Humour* was written, in fact, Jonson was in that year collaborating with Dekker in the writing of plays. *Henslowe's Diary* contains records (pp. 155, 156) of payments made to Jonson and Dekker jointly Aug. 10, 1599, and to Jonson, Chettle, Dekker, and "other Jentellman" Sept. 3, 1599. Critics who have found Dekker involved in the "War," at its close have assumed, apparently

The Metamorphosis of Pigmalion's Image and Certaine Satyres, by Marston, was entered in the Stationers' Register May 27, 1598 ; *The Scourge of Villanie*, by Marston, was entered Sept. 8, 1598 ; *Virgidemiarum*, by Hall, was entered March 30, 1598 ;[1] *Seven Satyres applied to the Week*, by Rankins, was entered May 3, 1598. In the Stationers' Register Marston is the third satirist, but priority of entry does not necessarily mean priority of publication, so that Marston's Satires may not have been third in date of publication. Be that as it may, the Satires of Rankins were comparatively unimportant, and attracted little attention compared to the more pretentious works of Hall and Marston, both of whom were "Scourgers" of the time, Marston calling his book *The Scourge of Villanie*, while Hall called his *Virgidemiarum*.[2] Marston was certainly the second "scourge" whatever position we assign him as a satirist.[3] In his Prologue Hall boldly announces :—

> I *first* adventure, follow me who list
> And be the *second* English satirist.[4]

---

without a particle of proof, that he was involved in it from the beginning, and that therefore, whenever we find in Jonson's plays a character satirizing Marston, we will find another character representing Dekker. We need quote here only one instance of such criticism. Dr. Robert Cartwright says: "Carlo Buffone, ' Thou Grand Scourge,' is of course Marston. . . . Fastidious Brisk is *consequently* Dekker." *Shakespeare and Jonson, Dramatic versus Wit Combats*, p. 16.

[1] Hall published his Satires in two parts : in 1597 *Virgidemiarum, Six Bookes ; First Three Bookes of Toothlesse Satyrs :* 1. *Poeticall ;* 2. *Academicall ;* 3. *Morall ;* in 1598 *Virgidemiarum : the Three Last Bookes of Byting Satyrs.*

[2] *Virga* was a rod or switch, and was used of the rods with which the lictors scourged criminals. *Virgidemia* is a comic word meaning a harvest of rods or stripes. The name of Hall's work is thus equivalent in meaning to that of Marston's.

[3] There were English satirists before Hall. Such satires as Hake's *Newes out of Paules Churchyarde,* 1567, Gascoigne's *Steel Glass,* 1576, and Lodge's *A Fig for Momus,* 1595, were well known before Hall wrote. Other satirists, earlier than Hall, might be mentioned.

[4] Hall may be entitled to some sort of priority, as his work was the first English satire in the general manner of Juvenal.

Virgidemiarum became popular ; and as Marston's work, similar in nature, appeared so soon after, it is probable that Hall's lines were remembered and applied to Marston, who was recognized generally as "the second English satirist" or "the Second Untruss." In calling Carlo the "Grand Scourge or Second Untruss of the Time," Jonson was using an appellation which, to the audience, was almost as definite as the name Marston would have been.

Puntarvolo says : "It is in the power of my purse to make him [Carlo] speak well or ill of me" (II. 1). Carlo is termed by Fastidious "a damned witty rogue" who "confounds with his similes" (II. 1) ; and in several other passages Carlo's similes are spoken of, the most important reference to them being Macilente's reproof, "You'll never leave your stabbing similes" (IV. 4). If we understand "simile" in its rhetorical sense, we find that Marston deserves the ridicule. His first reference to Jonson contains a comparison which is not above criticism : "Torquatus . . . that like some rotten stick in a troubled water hath gotte a great deale of barmie froth to stick to his sides."[1] Carlo's speeches abound in similes for which he is ridiculed by Fastidious in the epithet quoted above. The remark of Fastidious is occasioned by Carlo's statement concerning Cinedo, "He looks like a colonel of the Pigmies horse, or one of these motions in a great antique clock" (II. 1). Carlo's "vulgar phrase" (Marston's works are marred by coarse language) is

---

Rev. Thomas Corser says: "Marston has, till very lately, been usually styled the second English satirist, Bishop Hall being considered the first; he is mentioned by Charles Fitzgeffrey as contesting the palm of priority and merit in satire with Hall, in his *Affaniae*, or three books of Epigrams in Latin, published at Oxford in 1601 : —

. . . Satirarum proxima primae,
Primaque, fas primas si numerare duas.

And he is alluded to as such by Warton and other more modern writers." *Collectanea Anglo-Poetica*, IX. 13.

[1] "To those that Seeme Judiciall Perusers," *The Scourge of Villanie*.

very distasteful to Fastidious. Carlo says that Deliro "looks like one of the Patricians of Sparta," and Puntarvolo "looks like a shield of brawn at Shrove-tide" (IV. 4). To this Macilente replies, "Come, you 'll never leave your stabbing similes; I shall have you aiming at me with 'em by and by" (IV. 4). Carlo does aim at Macilente with a simile when he speaks of "lean bald-rib Macilente, that salt villain, plotting some mischievous device and lies a soaking in their frothy humours like a dry crust, till he has drunk 'em all up" (V. 4). The most severe attack on Marston as a man is the repeated reference to his treachery and double dealing. Marston was a gentleman as regards birth, his father being a Counsellor of the Middle Temple. When Sogliardo procures a coat of arms Carlo gives him advice about how to conduct himself as a gentleman. Jonson puts into the speech of Carlo a severe arraignment of Marston.

Carlo (to Sogliardo). Nay, look you, sir, now you are a gentleman, you must carry a more exalted presence, change your mood and habit to a more austere form; be exceeding proud, stand upon your gentility, and scorn every man; speak nothing humbly, never discourse under a nobleman, though you never saw him but riding to the Star Chamber, it 's all one. Love no man; trust no man; speak ill of no man to his face; nor well of any man behind his back. Salute fairly on the front, and wish them hanged upon the turn. Spread yourself upon his bosom publicly, whose heart you would eat in private. These be principles, think on them.[1]

The sentiments of this speech are repeated in the following words of Carlo :—

Tut, a man must keep time in all; I can oil my tongue when I meet him next, and look with a good sleek forehead; 't will take away all soil of suspicion, and that 's enough: what Lynceus can see my heart? Pish, the title of a friend! it 's a vain idle thing, only venerable among fools: you shall not have one that has any opinion of wit affect it.[2]

---

[1] III. 1. [2] IV. 4.

We have a remarkable scene (V. 4) referring undoubtedly to some actual incident, as is shown by the question of Mitis, "Whom should he [Carlo] personate in this?" Carlo, alone in a room at the Mitre, is represented with two wine cups, personating two men, who, after drinking healths, quarrel and overturn the table. They pledge "that honourable Countess" and also "the Count Frugale," who is mentioned by Fastidious as one of his friends (II. 1). The pledge is drunk by Carlo kneeling.[1] When Macilente enters he tells Carlo to ridicule the others when they come. Carlo then utters words, which are in imitation of Marston's language: "Whoreson, strummel-patched, goggle-eyed grumbledories, gigantomachized." Carlo expresses the opinion that man resembles nothing so much as swine, and therefore "pork is your only feed." The climax of the play is reached when Puntarvolo seals up Carlo's mouth. When the constables arrive Carlo and Fastidious are arrested. This indicates that the men (Marston and Daniel) satirized as Carlo and Fastidious were the persons at whom the play was especially aimed.

Marston's first attack on Jonson consisted of ridicule of "new-minted epithets (as reall, intrinsecate, Delphicke)."[2] At his earliest opportunity, Jonson retorted by ridiculing Marston's "fustian." It is for this purpose that Clove and Orange, "mere strangers to the whole scope of our play," are introduced in the scene laid in the Middle Aisle of St. Paul's (III. 1). Orange is "nothing but salutations." The ridicule of Marston's vocabulary is contained in the following passage, in which *Histriomastix* is named:—

---

[1] Carlo = Anaides (*Cynthia's Revels*), of whom we are told, "He never kneels but to pledge healths" (II. 1). See discussion of Anaides, below. It was a common custom to drink healths kneeling. Allusions to it are found in Chapman's *May Day*, II. 1; Fletcher's *Coxcomb*, I. 5, and in a number of other plays.

[2] "To those that Seeme Judiciall Perusers," *The Scourge of Villanie*. See above, p. 4.

Clove. Now, sir, whereas the ingenuity of the time, and the soul's synderisis are but embrions in nature, added to the paunch of Esquiline, and the intervallum of the zodiac, besides the ecliptic line being optic, and not mental, but by the contemplative and theoric part thereof, doth demonstrate to us the vegetable circumference, and the ventosity of the tropics, and whereas our intellectual or mincing capreal (according to the metaphysicks) as you may read in Plato's *Histriomastix* — you conceive me, sir?

Orange. O lord, sir!

Clove. Then coming to the pretty animal, as reason long since is fled to animals, you know, or indeed for the more modelizing, or enamelling, or rather diamondizing of your subject, you shall perceive the hypothesis, or galaxia (whereof the meteors long since had their initial inceptions and notions), to be merely Pythagorical, mathematical, and aristocratical — For, look you, sir, there is ever a kind of concinnity and species — Let us turn to our former discourse, for they mark us not.[1]

---

[1] The common error concerning Dekker's connection with the "War" has led some critics to identify Clove and Orange with Marston and Dekker. Dr. Brinsley Nicholson says: "With regard to the parts of Clove and Orange, who, as Cordatus says, 'are mere strangers to the whole scope of our play,' the extravagant diction of John Marston was without a doubt ridiculed in Clove's fustian phrases, while to every appearance Thomas Dekker was ridiculed as Orange." (*Ben Jonson,* ed. Brinsley Nicholson, Mermaid Series, I. 110.) Simpson accepts the opinion of Dr. Nicholson (*The School of Shakspere,* II. 5). It needs no long argument to show that both of these identifications are incorrect although Marston is ridiculed. Carlo (Marston) is on the stage when Clove utters the fustian. Nothing is said of Orange that can be applied to Dekker, with whom, moreover, Jonson had at this time no quarrel. (See note above, p. 46.)

Of the fustian words used by Clove we find that Marston uses the following: in *Histriomastix,* zodiac, ecliptic, tropic, mathematical, demonstrate (I. 1), paunch of Esquiline (III. 4); in *The Scourge of Villanie,* synderisis, Sat. VIII. (Emulo's use of "synderisis of soul" is ridiculed, *Patient Grissil,* III. 2); mincing capreal, Sat. XI.; capreal, Sat. I.; circumference, Sats. VI., X.; intellectual, "To Detraction," Sats. IV., VII., VIII., XI.; contemplation (not contemplative) Sats. VIII., XI.; Pythagoran (not Pythagorical) Sat. III. (Emulo is ridiculed for using "Diogenicall," *Patient Grissil,* II. 1); "diamondize" and "modelize" seem to be in ridicule of the forming of verbs by adding "ize" as Marston does (cf. idolatrize, Sat. VIII., also Brisk's use of "sinewize" and "arterize," III. 1, and Juniper's "pilgrimize," *Case is Altered,* II. 4). "Ingenuity" is used by Brisk and ridiculed by Macilente, III. 3. The vocabularies of Emulo (*Patient Grissil*) and Brisk (both of whom are probably satires on Daniel) are ridiculed, and some of their words are used by Clove and termed "fustian," so that Marston may not be the only writer whose language is here attacked.

Fastidious Brisk is not subjected to the bitter personal abuse that is showered upon Carlo Buffone, but he is none the less held up to ridicule for his devotion to dress, and his obsequious attendance upon ladies of the court. He is a courtier, and in this character Jonson ridicules the poet Daniel.[1] He is described thus: —

> A neat, spruce, affecting courtier, one that wears clothes well, and in fashion; practiseth by his glass, how to salute; speaks good remnants, notwithstanding the base viol and tobacco; swears tersely, and with variety; cares not what lady's favour he belies, or great man's familiarity; a good property to perfume the boot of a coach. He will borrow another man's horse to praise, and backs him as his own. Or, for a need, on foot can post himself into credit with his merchant, only with the gingle of his spur, and the jerk of his wand.

This character is drawn in ridicule of the absurd customs of the gallants, but also of an individual who bears a striking resemblance to Master Mathew in *Every Man in his Humour*, and Emulo in *Patient Grissil*. Cordatus describes Fastidious as a "fresh, Frenchified courtier ... as humorous as quick-silver" (I. 1). Throughout the play Fastidious is ridiculed for boasting of his intimacy with the nobility and his familiarity with court life. His flattery of ladies and his exquisite clothes are ridiculed. He boasts of his horses (II. 1). Carlo ridicules Fastidious' use of "arride" (II. 1), and Macilente ridicules the use of "ingenuity" for "wit" (III. 3). Fastidious is ridiculed whenever he appears, and when he boasts of his court friends, "Count Frugale, Signior Illustre, Signior Luculento[2] and a sort of 'em," Carlo remarks: "There's ne'er a one of these but might lie a week on the rack ere they could bring forth his name" (II. 1). Puntarvolo asks Fastidious whether he knows

---

[1] Mr. Sidney Lee states that Jonson ridiculed Lyly in the character of Fastidious Brisk. *Dictionary of National Biography*, s. v. John Lyly, p. 331. Allusion was made above (note, p. 47) to the identification of Fastidious Brisk with Dekker.

[2] With whom he fought the duel described in IV. 4.

"our court star there, that planet of wit Madonna Saviolina." Fastidious replies that she is his mistress, and that he has her scarf, or riband, or feather (II. 1). Madonna Saviolina is perhaps the same as Mathew's Madonna Hesperida.[1] She is probably the *Delia* of Daniel.[2]

Carlo and Fastidious dislike each other, and Carlo says of Fastidious : —

A gull, a fool, no salt in him 'i the earth, man: he looks like a fresh salmon kept in a tub; he'll be spent shortly. His brain's lighter than his feather already, and his tongue more subject to lye, than that is to wag : he sleeps with a musk-cat every night, and walks all day hanged in pomander chains for penance ; he has his skin tanned in civet, to make his complexion strong, and the sweetness of his youth lasting in the sense of his sweet lady ; a good empty puff.[3]

Fastidious is ridiculed constantly for his fine clothes. He thinks that "rich apparel hath strange virtues" (II. 2). He declares : —

I had three suits in one year made three great ladies in love with me ; I had other three undid three gentlemen in imitation ; and other three gat three other gentlemen widows of three thousand pound a year.

Jonson attacks Daniel's poetry in a passage (III. 1.) in which Fastidious is made to use expressions taken from *The Complaint of Rosamond*.

Fast. Good Signior Macilente, if this gentleman, Signior Deliro, furnish you, as he says he will, with clothes, I will bring you, to-morrow by this time, into the presence of the most divine and acute lady in court : you shall see *sweet silent rhetoric*, and *dumb eloquence* speaking in her eye.

---

[1] *Every Man in his Humour* (quarto), V. 1.
[2] Nashe dedicated *The Terrours of the Night* to Mistress Elizabeth Carey, 'sole daughter' of Sir George Carey, Knight. "Miraculous," says Nashe, "is your wit, and so is acknowledged by the wittiest poets of our age, who have vowed to enshrine you as their second Delia." Mr. Fleay identifies Elizabeth Carey with Daniel's *Delia*, and says: "The first Delia was Queen Elizabeth." *Chronicle of the English Drama*, I. 86.
[3] II. 1.

Gifford notes this ridicule of Daniel's expressions used in the following passage : —

> Ah, Beauty, Syren, fair enchanting good,
> *Sweet silent rhetoric* of persuading eyes,
> *Dumb eloquence*, whose power doth move the blood,
> More than the words or wisdom of the wise [1]

It is possible that Daniel's sonnets, while not quoted, may have been in Jonson's mind, when, to an absurd wish of Fastidious that he might be the viol on which his mistress plays, Macilente remarks : "I like such tempers well as stand before their mistresses with fear and trembling, and before their Maker like impudent mountains." There are several passages in which Macilente declares that Fastidious is not known at court. Fallace, who favors Fastidious, attributes these statements of Macilente to envy (IV. 1.), which was probably the real cause of Jonson's hostility to Daniel.[2] The facts concerning Daniel correspond in general with what we are told of Fastidious and his connection with ladies of the court.[3]

---

[1] *The Complaint of Rosamond.* Sir John Davies has an epigram on Daniel's "silent eloquence," *In Dacum*, 45 : —

> Dacus with some good colour and pretence
> Tearmes his loves beautie silent eloquence,
> For she doth lay more colours on her face
> Than even Tully used, his speech to grace.

The Complete Poems of Sir John Davies, ed. Grosart, II. 42.

Shakespeare's Sonnet 23 speaks of "eloquence and dumb presagers" of "silent love," which Mr. Fleay thinks is a hit at this passage of Daniel's. *Chronicle of the English Drama*, II. 215.

[2] See above, p. 13.

[3] Daniel was tutor to William Herbert, and lived at Wilton, the seat of his pupil's father. With Mary, Countess of Pembroke, Sir Philip Sidney's sister and young Herbert's mother, Daniel was on terms of intimacy. Later he became tutor to Anne, daughter of Margaret, Countess of Cumberland. The dedications of many of his poems show that he was intimate with the nobility. Daniel is said traditionally to have succeeded Spenser as Laureate in 1599, the year in which this play was produced. This fact may have a close connection with the attack on Daniel as Fastidious Brisk.

Fastidious describes a duel which he fought with Signior Luculento (IV. 4).[1] As the cause of the duel was "the same that sundered Agamemnon and great Thetis' son," and as Daniel, in his sonnets to *Delia*, 68 and 69, intimates that he had been wronged, it is possible that Luculento may be Lord Berkeley, whom Elizabeth Carey (identified as *Delia* by Mr. Fleay) married.[2] Fastidious is arrested with Carlo (IV. 4), and is visited, in the counter, by Fallace and Macilente. The latter remarks, "This it is to kiss the hand of a Countess, to have her coach sent for you," etc., referring to the boasts that Fastidious had made. We cannot identify the Countess with whom Fastidious was acquainted, but the career of Daniel would indicate that either the Countess of Pembroke or the Countess of Cumberland might possibly be alluded to.[3]

The sole ambition of Fungoso seems to be to dress like Fastidious. Fungoso is described as —

> The son of Sordido, and a student : one that has revelled in his time, and follows the fashion afar off, like a spy. He makes it the whole bent of his endeavours to wring sufficient means from his wretched father, to put him in the courtier's cut, at which he earnestly aims, but so unluckily, that he still lights short a suit.

Fungoso is godson of Puntarvolo. He studies law and is a gentleman (II. 1). Pretending to need law books, Fungoso obtains money from his father and spends it on clothes (II. 1). His sister Fallace is wife of Deliro, the citizen. Fungoso is dunned for bills by his tailor, shoemaker, and haberdasher (IV. 5), but succeeds in putting them off. His expensive habits of dress get him into debt, so that he is said to keep a

---

[1] This duel is similar to that between Emulo and Owen in *Patient Grissil*, III. 2. See below.

[2] *Chronicle of the English Drama*, I. 86. Mr. Fleay identifies Luculento with Drayton. *Ibid.*, p. 361. Luculento is mentioned in only one other passage, and then by Fastidious as being a gentleman of the court, II. 1.

[3] cf. *Dictionary of National Biography*, s. v. Samuel Daniel, pp. 25. 26.

tailor, "in place of a page, to follow him still" (IV. 5). After Carlo and Fastidious have been arrested (V. 4), Fungoso is discovered under a table and is made responsible for the bill. He is constantly ridiculed for having such fine clothes and no money with which to pay for them. Deliro pays the bill at the tavern for Fungoso (V. 6). The reference to the tailor's bill which Fungoso was unable to pay is, in itself, almost sufficient to identify him with Lodge, who was notorious for having been arrested in 1595 at the instigation of R. Topping, of the Strand, tailor. There are extant several documents which deal with the lawsuit concerning this bill. They date from 1595 to 1598. Lodge fled "beyond seas," and Henslowe, who had gone bail for him, refused to pay the bail or to disclose Lodge's hiding-place. Henslowe finally agreed to pay, and decision was rendered against him.[1] When Lodge published *A Fig for Momus*, 1595, the title-page bore the name of the author as "T. L. of Lincolne's Inne, Gent." We find in Lodge's study of law the original of Fungoso's study of law, but Lodge, like Fungoso, did not persevere in the law. When Fungoso hides under the table (V. 6) we have, perhaps, an allusion to Lodge's hiding during the trouble with the tailor. It is not impossible that the numerous references to a "suit" and to Fungoso's being "short a suit" may have a double meaning and include the lawsuit. Fungoso imitates and praises Brisk. Lodge imitated and praised Daniel.[2] Fungoso is at court in V. 2.

---

[1] For a summary of the facts concerning this lawsuit, see Mr. Fleay's *Chronicle of the English Drama*, II. 46. Mr. Edmund W. Gosse seems inclined to doubt that it was the poet Lodge who was concerned in this suit. *The Complete Works of Thomas Lodge*, printed for the Hunterian Club, 1883, "Memoir of Thomas Lodge," I. 30.

[2] In 1592 Daniel published *Delia, contayning certayne Sonnets: with the Complaint of Rosamond*, and in the next year Lodge published a book in many respects similar to Daniel's, entitled, *Phillis: honoured with Pastorall Sonnets, Elegies and Amorous Delights, whereunto is annexed the Tragicall Complaynt of Elstred*.

Macilente, who appears in the Induction as Asper, the author, is the first of the pictures of himself that Jonson is famous for having drawn. Asper is described as being —

of an ingenious and free spirit, eager, and constant in reproof, without fear controlling the world's abuses. One whom no servile hope of gain or frosty apprehension of danger, can make to be a parasite, either to time, place or opinion.

Macilente, the character which Asper assumes in the play, is —

A man well-parted, a sufficient scholar, and travelled : who, wanting that place in the world's account which he thinks his merit capable of, falls into such an envious apoplexy, with which his judgment is so dazzled and distasted, that he grows violently impatient of any opposite happiness in another.

The Induction, with Asper and his friends, Mitis and Cordatus, as the speakers, contains Jonson's bold announcement of the purpose of his play and his defiance of the critics.

> I fear no mood stamped in a private brow,
> When I am pleased t' unmask a public vice.

Asper is warned by Mitis and Cordatus that he will stir up antagonism and produce no good result. He replies to this in terms of haughty defiance of the world. When Asper is about to leave the stage he says : —

That Lodge had Daniel in mind in writing this book is shown by the opening poem, *Induction*, in which occur these lines : —

> Kiss *Delia's* hand for her sweet prophet's sake,
> Whose not affected, but well couched tears
> Have power, have worth, a marble minde to shake;
> Whose fame no Iron-age, or time outweares!
> Then lay you down in *Phillis'* lappe and sleepe,
> Untill she weeping read and reading weepe.

Lodge's *A Fig for Momus*, 1595, contained an *Eclogue* (No. 4) to Samuel Daniel. Jonson has combined the tailor's bill and Lodge's imitation of Daniel in Fungoso's imitation of Fastidious Brisk's clothes.

> Now gentlemen I go
> To turn an actor and a humorist,
> Where, ere I do resume my present person,
> We hope to make the circles of your eyes
> Flow with distilled laughter : if we fail
> We must impute it to this only chance
> Art hath an enemy called ignorance.

Surely this is no way to win the favour of an audience! Jonson had undoubtedly been subjected to much harsh criticism, as is shown by the tone of this Induction, and we look forward to the play itself, knowing that it is to be a reply to his critics. Throughout the play Macilente occupies the position of critic, and is not intimately connected with the plot, many of his speeches being "asides" which reveal to us the relationship which Jonson sustained to some of his contemporaries satirized in the play.

Carlo tells Sogliardo that Macilente is both a scholar and a soldier, which was true of Jonson. Carlo describes Macilente (I. 1) as —

> a lean mungrel, he looks as if he were chop-fallen with barking at other men's good fortunes ; 'ware how you offend him ; he carries oil, and fire in his pen, will scald where it drops ; his spirit is like powder, quick, violent ; he'll blow a man up with a jest : I fear him worse than a rotten wall does the cannon ; shake an hour after at the report.

This passage may have reference to the impression made by Jonson's earlier plays *Every Man in his Humour* and *The Case is Altered*.

Deliro admires Macilente and tells Fastidious (II. 2) that Macilente is a scholar and travelled, to which Brisk replies "He should get him clothes. . . . An he had good clothes I'd carry him to court with me tomorrow." Allusion to Jonson's shabby clothes is frequent throughout the plays concerned in "The War of the Theatres." In the same scene (II. 2) Macilente says : "Would my father had left me but a good face for my portion," a reference to Jonson's "rocky face"[1] ridiculed by his enemies.

When Macilente, in the presence of Fallace (IV. 1), makes a speech about Fastidious, "Alas the poor fantastic, etc.," she attributes to envy the hostility to Fastidious. In IV. 4, Macilente says that he was with Fastidious at court. Macilente poisons Puntarvolo's dog (V. 1), and discovers Fungoso under the table (V. 4). Macilente is the means of putting out of his humour every other character. Having succeeded in punishing almost all the other characters, except Deliro, who was his friend, Macilente makes his final speech in a style characteristic of Jonson.

Shift is another version of Bobadil. He is the subject of Epigram XII.[2] and is thus described in the "characters" : —

> A thread-bare shark ; one that never was a soldier, yet lives upon lendings. His profession is skeldring and odling, his bank Paul's, and his warehouse Picthatch. Takes up single testons upon oaths, till doomsday. Falls under executions of three shillings, and enters into five-groat bonds. He waylays the reports of services, and cons them without book, damning himself he came new from them, when all the while he was taking the diet in the bawdy-house, or lay pawned in his chamber for rent and victuals. He is of that admirable and happy memory, that he will salute one for an old acquaintance that he never saw in his life before. He usurps upon cheats quarrels and robberies, which he never did, only to get him a name. His chief exercises are, taking the whiff, squiring a cockatrice, and making privy searches for imparters.

---

[1] " My mountain belly and my rocky face," *My Picture left in Scotland.* The " mountain belly " was a later acquisition, for Jonson is in this play "lean Macilente," and "a rank, raw-boned Anatomy," IV. 4.

[2] Epigram XII. says of Shift, " His whole revenue is, God pays." In *The London Prodigal,* II. 3, we are told : —

> But there be some that bear a soldier's form
> That swear by him they never think upon,
> Go swaggering up and down from house to house,
> Crying, God pays all.

We learn from the play that Shift is a pimp, "the rarest superficies of a humour; he comes every morning to empty his lungs in Pauls" (III. 1). When he first appears he is about to post, in the middle aisle of Paul's, two bills, in one of which he offers his services as gentleman-usher to any gentlewoman who may be in need of such an attendant; in the other he offers his services to a young gentleman as an instructor in the most "gentlemanlike use of tobacco" (III. 1). As the result of this latter notice, Shift becomes the instructor of Sogliardo.

Shift appears in the aisle of Paul's "expostulating with his rapier," which, he declares, has travelled with him "the best part of France and the Low Country," in Lord Leicester's time (III. 1).[1] Shift's wonderful exploits are described by Sogliardo (IV. 4) but Puntarvolo makes Shift confess that all his boasting has been nothing but lies (V. 3). Sogliardo, who witnesses the humbling of Shift, dismisses him with contempt.[2]

Sogliardo is described in the "characters" as —

an essential clown, brother to Sordido, yet so enamoured of the name of a gentleman that he will have it, though he buys it. He comes up every term to learn to take tobacco, and see new motions. He is in his kingdom when he can get himself into company where he may be well laughed at.

He is ridiculed in the play and is introduced at court (V. 2) by Puntarvolo, who describes him ironically as being

exceedingly valiant, an excellent scholar, and so exactly travelled, that he is able, in discourse, to deliver you a model of any prince's court in the world; speaks the languages with that purity of phrase, and facility of accent, that it breeds astonishment; his wit the most exuberant, and, above wonder, pleasant, of all that ever entered the concave of this ear. . . . But that which transcends all, lady: he doth so peerlessly imitate any manner of person for gesture, action, passion.

---

[1] Brainworm makes similar boasts of military service, and sells his rapier to Master Stephen, *Every Man in his Humour*, II. 2.

[2] Bobadil was humbled by Downright, *Every Man in his Humour*, IV. 5.

Carlo, who is instructing Sogliardo "in all the rare qualities, humours, and compliments of a gentleman" (I. 1), gives as the first requisite, that Sogliardo "must give over housekeeping in the country, and live altogether in the city" (I. 1). Sogliardo must have a coat of arms, and Carlo tells him how to procure one (I. 1).[1] Sogliardo obtains a coat of arms from the herald's office at a cost of thirty pounds (III. 1). His crest is described as "a boar without a head, rampant." Carlo's comment is —

> I commend the herald's wit, he has decyphered him well: a swine without a head, without brain, wit, anything indeed, ramping to gentility.

The escutcheon is —

> Gyrony of eight pieces: azure and gules; between three plates, a chevron engrailed checquy, or, vert and ermins; on a chief argent, between two ann'lets sable, a boar's head, proper.[2]

---

[1] Sogliardo resembles in some respects Master Stephen in *Every Man in his Humour*. Stephen, like Sogliardo, is a countryman who wishes to make "a blaze of gentry to the world." Stephen employs Bobadil to teach him "whatsoever is incident to a gentleman" (III. 1). Sogliardo and Stephen are both rich. The former is advised by Carlo to turn "four or five hundred acres" of his best land into apparel (I. 1), while the latter declares, "I have a very pretty living of my own, hard by here" (I. 1). It may seem fanciful, but it is perhaps worth mentioning that Sogliardo is called "that swine," while Stephen's abode was Hogs-den.

[2] Mr. Fleay says: "Sogliardo's arms, 'on a chief argent between two ann'lets sable, a boar's head proper,' indicate Burbadge (*Boar-badge*); badge (*bague*) being a ring, garland, or annulet." *Shakespeare Manual*, p. 312. Mr. Fleay says also: "In V. 4, I believe that 'hog' and 'usurous cannibals' refers to the Boar-badges, and that all the allusions to swine in this play do likewise; but I do not expect the reader to agree with me." *Chronicle of the English Drama*, I. 361. Sordido is "a Burbadge, some country relative of Richard Burbadge" (*ibid.*, p. 360). This interpretation of the coat of arms is plausible, and were there no other considerations, might be accepted. Sordido and Sogliardo, if Burbadges at all, must have been relatives of Richard Burbadge. Neither of them was Richard Burbadge. This play, like its predecessor, was acted by the Chamberlain's men, and Richard Burbadge, as the folio informs us, took part in both plays. It is improbable that Jonson, who was writing for the Chamberlain's company, would have satirized, by allusions to hogs, swine, and boars' heads, either the man or the

In any attempt to identify Sogliardo we must consider also his brother, Sordido, who is described by Macilente (I. 1) as "Sordido the farmer, a boor, and brother to that swine [Sogliardo] was here." Sordido's "character" is —

A wretched hob-nailed chuff, whose recreation is reading of almanacks; and felicity, foul weather. One that never prayed but for a lean dearth, and ever wept in a fat harvest.

Sordido is rich, but "like a boisterous whale, swallows the poor" (I. 1). He will not bring his corn to market though the people starve. He is "cause to the curse of the poor" (III. 2). He hangs himself because "his prognostication has not kept touch with him" (III. 2), but is cut down by "rustics" whose curses upon him effect a change in his character. What we are told of Sordido agrees in many respects with what we know of Philip Henslowe, the "old pawnbroking, stage-managing, bear-baiting usurer," whose company of actors was at this time the chief rival of the Chamberlain's men. Henslowe owned a great deal of property in Southwark, where he lived.[1] He might properly be spoken of as a "boor" or countryman, for his early years were spent in the country.[2]

In connection with the coat of arms, "boar's head," "swine," and similar allusions in the play, it is interesting to note the

---

relatives or the name of the man who was the chief actor in the company, and upon whom the success of the play so largely depended. No Burbadges of whom we have any knowledge are in any way to be identified with Sordido and Sogliardo.

[1] In a passage which probably refers to Henslowe, Chettle denounces landlords who are harsh to poor tenants. *Kind Hartes Dreame. Shakspere Allusion-Books*, Pt. I., ed. C. M. Ingleby. New Shakspere Society Publications. *Henslowe's Diary* contains numerous entries recording payments of rent by his tenants.

[2] Henslowe was a native of Sussex, and was servant to Woodward, bailiff to Viscount Montague, whose property included Battle Abbey and Cowdray, in Sussex, and Montague House in Southwark. Henslowe settled in Southwark in 1577, in St. Saviour's Parish. See article " Philip Henslowe," by William Rendle, in *The Genealogist*, 1890; also *Dictionary of National Biography, s. v.* Philip Henslowe.

fact that Henslowe owned the notorious as well as famous Boar's Head tavern in Southwark,[1] and that his brother-in-law ("that swine was here"?) was Ralph Hogge, an iron-founder at Buxted. There may or may not be any significance in these facts.

The language used by Puntarvolo is an object of ridicule in the absurd scene (II. 2) in which he converses with his wife. The language is similar to that used by Amorphus in *Cynthia's Revels*. Puntarvolo is "a gentleman of exceeding good humour."

He loves dogs and hawks and his wife well; he has a good riding face and he can sit a great horse; he will taint a staff well at tilt; when he is mounted he looks like the sign of the George.

He has dialogues and discourses between his horse, himself, and his dog.[2]

Puntarvolo intends to travel, and lays a wager on his safe return. He says:—

I am determined to put forth some five thousand pound, to be paid me five for one, upon the return of myself and wife and my dog, from the Turk's court in Constantinople.[2]

---

[1] We know that Henslowe owned the Boar's Head tavern in 1604 from the following entry in his diary: "The Bores Heade tenantes, as foloweth, begenynge at crystmase laste, 1604." *Henslowe's Diary*, p. 265; see also p. 266. Henslowe owned much property in the immediate neighborhood of the Boar's Head tavern as early as 1584-85, and it seems altogether probable that he owned the Boar's Head tavern either wholly or in part as early as 1597 or 1598, although investigation has failed to disclose any positive proof that he did. W. H. Atkins, Esq., Clerk of the Board of Works for the St. Saviour's district (to whom, as also to the Rev. W. Thompson, Rector of St. Saviour's, the writer acknowledges his indebtedness for information on this point) thus answers a question concerning the record of ownership of the old tavern: "You ask whether there is an office in which deeds are registered. There is none for Surrey, but there is a registry for the County of Middlesex. If any deeds relating to the inn are in existence they are probably in the hands of private individuals: but titles on purchase or sale are now, I understand, seldom traced back more than thirty years, and this is inimical to the preservation of old deeds."

[2] II. 1.

Puntarvolo has travelled as far as Paris, and speaks French and Italian. Carlo describes Puntarvolo as a "dull stiff knight" who "has a good knotty wit." He is, says Carlo, —

a good tough gentleman: he looks like a shield of brawn at Shrove-tide, out of date, and ready to take his leave; or a dry pole of ling upon Easter-eve, that has furnished the table all Lent, as he has done the city this last vacation.[1]

Puntarvolo goes to court and leaves his dog in the care of a groom. Macilente poisons the dog (V. 1). Antagonism is developed between Puntarvolo and Carlo. It is Puntarvolo who calls Carlo "thou Grand Scourge or Second Untruss of the Time" (II. 1), and who seals up Carlo's mouth in the tavern scene (V. 4). Puntarvolo is evidently the same person as Amorphus in *Cynthia's Revels*. Anthony Monday is probably the man ridiculed in these two characters, but the proofs of this will be postponed until the facts concerning Amorphus have been set forth.[2]

Deliro, the friend of Macilente, is described in the "characters" as—

A good doting citizen, who, it is thought, might be of the Common Council for his wealth; a fellow sincerely besotted on his own wife, and so rapt with a conceit of her perfections, that he simply holds himself unworthy of her. And, in that hood-winked humour lives more like a suitor than a husband; standing in as true dread of her displeasure, as when he first made love to her. He doth sacrifice two-pence in juniper to her every morning before she rises, and wakes her with villainous out-of-tune music, which she out of her contempt (though not out of her judgment) is sure to dislike.

---

[1] IV. 4.

[2] "Puntarvolo with his dog may be Sir John Harington (for the dog, see the engraved title of his *Ariosto*)." *Chronicle of the English Drama*, I. 360. Mr. Fleay suggests also that Puntarvolo is the same person as Amorphus, and that Amorphus is Barnaby Rich (*ibid.*, p. 363). This identification is discussed below. Dr. Cartwright thought that Puntarvolo was a caricature of Lyly. *Shakespeare and Jonson, Dramatic versus Wit Combats*, p. 16.

Deliro entertains Macilente at his house and promises to provide Macilente with clothes in which to appear at court with Fastidious (II. 2). Deliro's chief claim to distinction seems to rest on his having a shrew for a wife. He pays the bill at the tavern for Fungoso (V. 6) and finally discovers Fallace's passion for Fastidious (V. 7). Macilente criticises Fallace, but Deliro refuses to believe anything ill of her. She is the daughter of Sordido and sister of Fungoso, whose attempts to imitate Brisk she approves and aids. Deliro has entered into three actions against Fastidious (V. 7), and holds mortgages on all the lands of Fastidious (IV. 1).

Deliro and Fallace are probably the same persons as the Citizen and his wife (*Cynthia's Revels*), and Albius and Chloe (*Poetaster*).[1]

The scene (II. 2) in which Deliro and Fallace display their lack of harmony, and Fallace shows her fondness for Fastidious, was intended as personal satire, as is clearly indicated by the comments of Mitis and Cordatus. Cordatus says of the interpretation of the scene : —

> Indeed there are a sort of these narrow-eyed decypherers, I confess, that will extort strange and abstruse meanings out of any subject, be it never so conspicuous and innocently delivered. But to such, where'er they sit concealed, let them know, the author defies them and their writing-tables ; and hopes no sound or safe judgment will infect itself with their contagious comments, who, indeed, come here only to pervert and poison the sense of what they hear and for nought else.

It has been thought that in *Every Man out of his Humour* (III. 1) Jonson has introduced an allusion to *Twelfth Night*. Mitis fears that objection will be made to Jonson's play : —

> That the argument of his comedy might have been of some other nature, as of a duke to be in love with a countess, and that countess to be in love

---

[1] Mr. Fleay thinks "Deliro, possibly Monday." *Chronicle of the English Drama*, I. 360. No reason for this conjecture is given.

with the duke's son, and the son to love the lady's waiting maid; some such cross wooing with a clown to their serving man, better than to be thus near and familiarly allied to the time.

There is some uncertainty as to the date of *Twelfth Night*,[1] but, even if it could be proved that it was produced before Jonson's play, the plot here suggested by Jonson is, as Gifford has shown, not sufficiently in accord with the plot of *Twelfth Night* to make the allusion certain. The remark of Mitis is really a reply to a possible objection to Jonson's characters, that they were not dukes and countesses, but simply ordinary people of the time. In this regard the characters in Jonson's plays are in contrast to those in the plays of many other Elizabethan dramatists.

[1] 1600–1 is the date usually accepted by critics at the present time.

V.

PATIENT GRISSIL AND JACK DRUM'S ENTERTAINMENT.

FOUR plays of Dekker have been thought by critics to have been connected with the quarrel between Jonson and Marston, viz., *The Shoemaker's Holiday*, *Old Fortunatus*, *Patient Grissil*, and *Satiromastix*. In regard to the last there can be no difference of opinion, as it was avowedly a reply to Jonson's Satirical Comedies, especially to *Poetaster*. Before treating of *Patient Grissil* it is necessary to notice the following statement concerning the first two of the plays mentioned:—

... on account of their connection with the quarrel between Jonson and Dekker and Marston ... it may be not out of place to mention that Dekker's *Shoemaker's Holiday* and *Old Fortunatus* also belong to the series of attacks to which Jonson was (as he tells us[1]) subject for three years before he made any retaliation.[2]

Although these plays contain personal satire, yet an examination of them has failed to reveal any attack on Jonson.

Several mistakes concerning Dekker's connection with the "War" have been mentioned.[3] There is no attack on Jonson in any play of Dekker's earlier than *Satiromastix* (1601), a play which Dekker was "hired" by Jonson's enemies to write. If there had been any earlier attack, Jonson would not have failed to refer to it, but would undoubtedly have retaliated by representing Dekker in some character in the earlier comedies.

---

[1] *Poetaster*, Apologetical Dialogue.
[2] *Shakespeare Manual*, F. G. Fleay, p. 277.
[3] Above, pp. 46, note, 51, note.

There is, however, no representation of Dekker, or allusion to any play of Dekker's, in Jonson's works earlier than *Poetaster* (1601), in which Dekker is represented as Demetrius, who is to write a play satirizing Horace (Jonson). Dekker and Jonson were collaborating at almost the very time at which Dekker's portions of *The Shoemaker's Holiday* and *Old Fortunatus* were probably written.[1]

Patient Grissil was written only in part by Dekker, the other writers being Chettle and Haughton, as Henslowe's entries show. It was completed and acted early in 1600, for Henslowe made a payment on the play as late as Dec. 29, 1599,[2] and on March 18, 1599 (old style), he paid forty shillings to stay the printing of the play.[3]

Emulo, with his absurd "gallimaufry of language," has been thought by some to be a caricature of Jonson, the duel between Emulo and Owen (III. 2)[4] having reference to Jonson's duel with Gabriel Spencer, and the mention of laths, lime, and hair (II. 1) being an allusion to Jonson's bricklaying.[5] Any one who reads the play carefully will see that Emulo resembles

---

[1] Henslowe bought from Dekker *The Gentle Craft* or *The Shoemaker's Holiday* for three pounds on July 15, 1599 (*Henslowe's Diary*, p. 154). Payments for *Old Fortunatus* were made to Dekker by Henslowe on November 9, 24, and 31 (*sic*), 1599 (*ibid.*, pp. 159, 160, 161). During August and September, 1599, Jonson was collaborating with Dekker in writing plays which Henslowe calls "pagge of plimothe" and "Robart the second, Kinge of Scottes tragedie" (*ibid.*, pp. 155, 156).

[2] Payments for *Patient Grissil* were made on Oct. 16, Dec. 19, 26, 28, 29, 1599. *Henslowe's Diary*, pp. 96, 158, 162.

[3] *ibid.*, p. 167. The quarto has this title-page: *The Pleasant Comodie of Patient Grissil. As it hath beene sundrie times lately plaid by the right honorable the Earle of Nottingham (Lord high Admirall) his servants. London. Imprinted for Henry Rocket, and are to be solde at the long Shop under S. Mildred's Church in the Poultry*, 1603.

[4] The quarto is not divided into acts and scenes. The references here are to the divisions made by Collier in the Shakespeare Society reprint of the play.

[5] "Dekker avenged his friend [Marston, who had recently been satirized as Carlo Buffone] by introducing Jonson as Emulo, the lath, lime, and hair man in *Patient Grissil*." *The North British Review*, July, 1870, p. 402.

Jonson in no particular, and that the laths, lime, and hair are mentioned because Emulo's boot has been called a "wall" to "save his shins."

Mr. Fleay has probably interpreted this character correctly as a representation of Samuel Daniel, who had been satirized by Jonson as Fastidious Brisk.[1] Emulo, like Fastidious Brisk, is a courtier and is characterized (II. 1) by Farneze as —

one of those changeable silk gallants, who, in a very scurvy pride, scorn all scholars and read no books but a looking-glass, and speak no language but "sweet lady" and "sweet signior," and chew between their teeth terrible words, as though they would conjure, as "compliment," and "projects," and "fastidious," and "capricious,"[2] and "misprision," and "the sintheresis of the soul" and such like raise-velvet terms.

Jonson makes Fastidious Brisk use some of the same words that are used by Emulo, and "the soul's synderisis," an expression of Clove's, is the same as "the sintheresis of the soul," used by Emulo. The "fustian" talked by Clove resembles the "gallimaufry of language" of Emulo. Concerning Clove we are told : —

He will sit you a whole afternoon sometimes in a bookseller's shop, reading the Greek, Italian, and Spanish, when he understands not a word of either ; if he had the tongues to his suits, he were an excellent linguist.[3]

Of Emulo it is said : —

My brisk spangled baby will come into a stationer's shop, call for a stool and a cushion, and then asking for some Greek poet, to him he falls, and there he grumbles God knows what, but I 'll be sworn he knows not so much as one character of the tongue.[4]

---

[1] *Chronicle of the English Drama*, I, 97, note 1.
[2] Fastidious Brisk uses "capriciously," *Every Man out of his Humour*, II. 1.
[3] *Every Man out of his Humour*, III. 1.
[4] II. 1. The following passage in Dekker's *Guls Horne-booke* indicates that Clove and Emulo were only following the custom : " I could now fetch you about noone ... out of your chamber, and carry you with mee into Paules Churchyard ; where planting yourself in a Stationers shop, many instructions are to bee given

"Fastidious" is one of Emulo's words, and he is called "a brisk spangled baby." We are thus reminded of Jonson's representation of Daniel as Fastidious Brisk. When it is said that Emulo will "pull out a bundle of sonnets, written, and read them to ladies,"[1] there is, perhaps, an allusion to Daniel's *Delia*.

The duel between Emulo and Owen described in III. 2 is similar to that between Fastidious Brisk and Luculento described in *Every Man out of his Humour*, IV. 4, and they may have reference to the same incident. It is evident that Dekker had in mind the passage in Jonson's play. As both duels were about a woman and as Emulo and Fastidious Brisk are evidently the same person, it is possible that the woman may have been Delia (Lady Elizabeth Carey), and Owen and Luculento may be representations of Lord Berkeley her husband.[2]

Although no other character in *Patient Grissil* has been identified, yet the almost certain identity of Emulo with Daniel establishes a connection between this play and others concerned in "The War of the Theatres," and may show that Dekker, if at this time involved in the "war," was on Jonson's side, at least so far as to join in the attack on Daniel. We do not know positively what parts of *Patient Grissil* were written by Dekker and what by Chettle and Haughton.[3] The play was performed at the Rose by the Admiral's company.

---

you, what bookes to call for, how to censure of new bookes, how to mew at the old, how to looke in your tables and inquire for such and such Greeke, French, Italian or Spanish authors, whose names you have there, but whom your mother for pitty would not give you so much wit as to understand." *Dekker*, ed. Grosart, II. 265.

[1] II. 1.

[2] See Mr. Fleay's *Chronicle of the English Drama*, I. 86, 272.

[3] Mr. Fleay may be correct in his conjecture that Dekker "mainly wrote the scenes in which Laureo and Babulo (the characters not found in the old story) enter, and Chettle the Welsh scenes; Haughton the remainder, besides helping Dekker in his part." *Chronicle of the English Drama*, I. 271.

Jack Drum's Entertainment, or The Comedy of Pasquil and Katherine is, like *Histriomastix*, a play which was published anonymously, and is not published among Marston's plays by his editors. As in the case of *Histriomastix*, the unusual vocabulary employed indicates that Marston was the author.[1] The fact that Jonson, when attacking Marston as Crispinus,[2] ridicules passages in *Jack Drum*, is additional proof that Marston wrote it. The play was performed in 1600 (" 't is womens yeere,"[3] or leap-year) at Whitsuntide.

Marston probably refers to the attack made on him in the "fustian" conversation between Clove and Orange,[4] when he makes Planet say :—

> By the Lord, fustian, now I understand it : complement is as much as fustian.[5]

The adventure of Monsieur John fo de King, the licentious Frenchman, with the wife of Brabant Senior, corresponds almost exactly with the first of the "accidents strange" which Jonson related to Drummond.[6] It would be remarkable if, with all the bitter personality of these dramatic satires, there should be no allusion to Jonson's licentiousness, and it is therefore more than likely that the character of Monsieur John fo de King is an attack on Jonson.

It is possible that Jonson's duel and narrow escape from

---

[1] Dr. Brinsley Nicholson says, in a note on *Jack Drum* (*Notes and Queries*, Series 7, Vol. VII. p. 67), " I was happy to hear from my friend J. O. Halliwell-Phillipps ... that a MS. (*circa* 1620) gives unequivocal testimony to Marston's authorship of *Jack Drum's Entertainment*."

[2] *Poetaster*, V. 1.

[3] I. 1. The references are to the play as printed by Simpson in *The School of Shakspere*, II.

[4] *Every Man out of his Humour*, III. 1.

[5] III. l. 87.

[6] See above, p. 40.

hanging may be glanced at in the words of Monsieur John fo de King when he is hired by Mammon to kill Pasquil : —

> ... You see
> Mee kill a man, you see mee hang like de Bergullian.[1]

Attention has been called[2] to the necessity of revising the punctuation of the passage in the *Conversations with Drummond*, in which Jonson states that the beginning of the quarrel with Marston was that "Marston represented him in the stage." This statement could not refer to *Jack Drum*, for the date of that play is 1600, whereas the quarrel was bitter in 1599, when Jonson attacked Marston's *Histriomastix* and *Satires*, and Marston himself as Carlo Buffone. It has been shown[3] that *Histriomastix* is the play containing the first representation of Jonson by Marston. *Jack Drum* therefore contains Marston's second representation of Jonson. Although to us the character of Monsieur John fo de King does not seem to resemble Jonson, yet stage " business " and mimicry were probably introduced in presenting these plays, so that to the audience it was perfectly clear who was represented.

The other characters in *Jack Drum* have been identified in various ways. Simpson conjectured that Brabant Junior was Marston,[4] an identification which seems probable, especially in view of the allusion to small legs as a proof of gentility.

> *Winifride.* Indeed young Brabant is a proper man ;
> And yet his legs are somewhat of the least ;
> And, faith, a chittie, well-complexion'd face ;
> And yet it wants a beard : a good sweet youth ;
> And yet some say, he hath a valiant breath ;
> Of a good haire, but oh, his eyes, his eyes ![5]

Simpson thought Brabant Senior a caricature of Jonson,[6]

---

[1] II. 1. 180.
[2] Above, p. 40.
[3] Above, p. 41.
[4] *The School of Shakspere*, II. 128.
[5] I. ll. 227-232.
[6] *The School of Shakspere*, II. 130.

and in this opinion Mr. Bullen agrees.¹ This identification is based on the following remarks of Planet to Brabant Junior, alluding to Brabant Senior :—

> Deare Brabant, I doe hate these bumbaste wits,
> That are puft up with arrogant conceit
> Of their owne worth ; as if Omnipotence
> Had hoised them to such unequal'd height
> That they survai'd our spirits with an eye
> Onely create to censure from above :
> When good soules they doe nothing but reprove.²

There is no other resemblance between Brabant Senior and Jonson, and these lines are equally applicable to Hall, whom Mr. Fleay has identified with Brabant Senior, thus making the two Brabants represent the two satirists, Hall and Marston.³ The fact that Hall's satires appeared before Marston's, and that the two satirists were associated in the minds of the people, coupled with the censorious spirit of Brabant Senior and the praise of Brabant Junior, tends to prove Mr. Fleay's identification.

Sir Edward Fortune has been identified with Edward Alleyn, who was at that time building the Fortune Theatre. Mammon is a usurer. The passage in which Pasquil tears up the bonds suggests the possible identity of Mammon with Sordido, the miser in *Every Man out of his Humour*. Both are said to use almanacs and are hated by the people.⁴

It has been shown that Sordido is perhaps a representation of Henslowe,⁵ and it is possible that Mammon may have been intended for the same person. Alleyn was the son-in-law of

---

[1] *The Works of John Marston*, ed. Bullen, I. liv.
[2] IV. ll. 316-322.
[3] *Chronicle of the English Drama*, II. 74.
[4] Compare the last scene of Act III. of *Jack Drum* with what we are told of Sordido in *Every Man out of his Humour*, I. 1 and III. 2.
[5] Above, p. 62.

Henslowe, but in *Jack Drum* Mammon is the friend, "in hope" the son-in-law of Sir Edward Fortune.[1]

There is a scene in which Planet and the two Brabants criticise several poets: —

Brabant Junior.   Brother, how like you of our moderne wits?
                    How like you the new poet Mellidus?
Brabant Senior.   A slight bubling spirit, a corke, a huske.
Planet.   How like you Musus fashion in his carriage?
Brabant Senior.   O filthilie, he is as blunt as Paules.
Brabant Junior.   What thinke you of the lines of Decius?
                    Writes he not a good cordiall sappie stile?
Brabant Senior.   A surreinde jaded wit, but a rubbes on.
Planet.   Brabant, thou art like a paire of ballance,
                    Thou wayest all saving thy selfe.[2]

The comments of Brabant Senior are in keeping with the tone of Hall's Satires. Mellidus is probably Marston, who had evidently written the first part of *Antonio and Mellida*. The fact that we have in *Jack Drum* an allusion to *Antonio and Mellida*, and that in the latter play there is a reference to *Cynthia's Revels*,[3] indicates the order in which these three plays, all of the date 1600, were performed. Simpson conjectured that Musus, "as blunt as Paules," was "either Chapman, who, as Chettle says, 'finished sad Musæus' gracious song,' or Daniel, whom Drayton, in *Endimion and Phœbe*, 1594, calls 'the sweet Musæus of these times.'"[4] It is more likely that Daniel was meant by Musus, for the criticism seems to be more applicable to him than to Chapman. Decius is Drayton, who is called by that name in an epigram by Sir John Davies.[5]

---

[1] I. 1. 74.   [2] IV. II. 37-46.
[3] This reference to *Cynthia's Revels* will be discussed below in treating of *Antonio and Mellida*.
[4] *The School of Shakspere*, II. 131.
[5] In *Idea*, Sonnet XVIII, Drayton speaks of his Mistress as a "tenth" muse. To this Sir John Davies refers in the epigram: —

Mr. Fleay makes a number of guesses as to the identity of other characters in the play. "Timothy Tweedle seems very like Antony Monday, and Christopher Flawn I take to be Christopher Beeston. John Ellis, with his similes, is a gross caricature of John Lyly. . . . Pasquil is perhaps Nicholas Breton"[1] or Nashe. Simpson remarks that "Planet, to whom the sceptre of criticism seems to be tacitly conceded, one hopes may have been meant for Shakspere."[2] There seems to be no positive proof of the correctness of any of these conjectures.

In Decium.

Audacious painters have nine worthies made,
But Poet Decius more audacious farre,
Making his Mistresse march with men of warre
With title of tenth worthie doth her lade.
      Sir John Davies, ed. Grosart, II. 24.

[1] *Chronicle of the English Drama*, II. 74.
[2] *The School of Shakspere*, II. 131.

VI.

CYNTHIA'S REVELS.

MERELY as a play, *Cynthia's Revels* is perhaps the least interesting that Jonson wrote, but as a personal satire it has great interest on account of its directness. The object of the play was to satirize the same four men that were attacked in *Every Man out of his Humour*. They are probably the four to whom Dekker refers in the following lines in *Satiromastix*: —

> I wonder then, that of five hundred, foure
> Should all point with their fingers in one instant
> At one and the same man.[1]

That Dekker was not himself one of the four is indicated (as will be seen from the context) by the fact that it is Demetrius (Dekker) who speaks the lines. We have shown that in *Every Man out of his Humour* the men attacked were Marston, Daniel, Lodge, and Monday. In *Cynthia's Revels* these men are represented respectively as Anaides, Hedon, Asotus, and Amorphus; Crites is of course Jonson. The characters appear usually in pairs, Anaides and Hedon, and Asotus and Amorphus. These two pairs are not on good terms with each other, but are unanimous in their dislike of Crites. The female characters may be considered wholly allegorical, but they are none the less satirical as bearing the names of the follies which characterize their respective gallants.

---

[1] *The Dramatic Works of Thomas Dekker, now first collected with illustrative notes and a memoir of the author*, published by John Pearson, London, 1873, I. 198.

Cynthia's Revels has come down to us in two forms. The quarto (1601) probably gives the play as it was presented at court, and is much shorter than the folio (1616).[1]

Anaides (Marston) is closely associated with Hedon (Daniel) throughout the play, and together they plot against Crites (Jonson). In the Induction Anaides is spoken of as "the Impudent, a gallant." When Anaides first appears (II. 1) he has more oaths than he "knows how to utter." Mercury says that Anaides, although not a courtier, —

. . . has two essential parts of the courtier, pride and ignorance: marry, the rest come somewhat after the ordinary gallant. 'Tis Impudence itself, Anaides: one that speaks all that comes in his cheeks, and will blush no more than a sackbut. He lightly occupies the jester's room at the table,[2] and keeps laughter, Gelaia, a wench in page's attire, following him in place of a squire, whom he now and then tickles with some strange ridiculous stuff, uttered as his land came to him, by chance. He will censure or discourse of anything, but as absurdly as you would wish. His fashion is not to take knowledge of him that is beneath him in clothes.[3] He never drinks below the salt. He does naturally admire his wit that wears gold lace or tissue: stabs any man that speaks more contemptibly of the scholar than he.[4] He is a great proficient in all the illiberal sciences, as cheating, drinking, swaggering, whoring, and such like: never kneels but to pledge healths,[5] nor

---

[1] The citizen and his wife (V. 2) do not appear in the quarto, and the second of the games, "A thing done and who did it" (IV. 1), is likewise not in the quarto. The first two-thirds of the last act appeared in print for the first time in the folio. The play may have been "cut" for court presentation, giving us the text as printed in the quarto, or additions may have been made later, giving the text as printed in the folio. This play was first acted by the Chapel children at Blackfriars theatre in 1600. Jonson was no longer writing for the Chamberlain's company, by whom *Every Man in his Humour* and *Every Man out of his Humour* were presented.

[2] Anaides, "the jester," is the same man as Carlo Buffone (the buffoon) in *Every Man out of his Humour*. Both are Marston (see above, p. 46, note).

[3] Evidently referring to Marston's contempt for Jonson, whose coarse clothes were often ridiculed.

[4] The scholar was probably Jonson.

[5] Mention was made above (p. 50, note) of the connection between this statement and the passage (*Every Man out of his Humour*, V. 4) in which Carlo drinks a health kneeling. An interesting passage occurs in *A Yorkshire Tragedy* (I. 1): —

prays but for a pipe of pudding-tobacco. He will blaspheme in his shirt. The oaths which he vomits at one supper would maintain a town of garrison in good swearing a twelvemonth. One other genuine quality he has which crowns all these, and that is this: to a friend in want, he will not depart with the weight of a soldered groat lest the world might censure him prodigal, or report him a gull: marry, to his cockatrice, or punquetto, half a dozen taffata gowns or satin kirtles in a pair or two of months, why they are nothing.[1]

The character here described agrees with that of Carlo Buffone. The hostility of Anaides and Hedon to Crites is set forth at length in a scene (III. 2) which must have displeased the audience, who saw Crites in close consultation with Arete immediately after Anaides and Hedon had declared that they would "undo" Crites. Anaides suggests (III. 2) that they get Crites "in, one night, and make him pawn his wit for a supper" for the party, a proceeding which had probably been executed successfully on more than one occasion by Marston and his friends, as may perhaps be inferred from the title "Anaides of the ordinary," but more directly from the description of Carlo Buffone as "a good feast-hound or banquet-beagle, that will scent you out a supper some three miles off."[2]

Anaides tells Hedon to annoy Crites by attacking his works, and suggests the following plan:—

Approve anything thou hearest of his, to the received opinion of it; but if it be extraordinary, give it from him to some other whom thou more particularly affect'st; that's the way to plague him, and he shall never come

---

"*Sam.* . . . I'll teach you the finest humour to be drunk in; I learned it in London last week.

"*Both.* I' faith? Let's hear it.

"*Sam.* The bravest humour! 't would do a man good to be drunk in it; they call it knighting in London, when they drink upon their knees."

[1] Marston was attacked in this play for licentiousness; and in his next play, *Jack Drum*, produced probably immediately after this play of Jonson's, he retaliated by satirizing Jonson for licentiousness (see above, p. 71).

[2] "Character" of Carlo Buffone, prefixed to *Every Man out of his Humour.*

to defend himself. 'Slud. I'll give out all he does is dictated from other men, and swear it too, if thou'lt have me, and that I know the time and place where he stole it.[1]

The suggestion of Anaides probably indicates that this mode of attack on Jonson had been employed by his enemies, perhaps in reply to the accusations against Daniel made in *Every Man in his Humour* (IV. 1), where Master Mathew "utters nothing but stolen remnants," and filches "from the dead." It is this plan of Anaides that Mr. Fleay thinks "conclusive as to the identity of Anaides, and therefore of Carlo Buffone, with Demetrius (Dekker). 'I know the time and place where he stole it,' says Anaides; 'I know the authors from whence he has stole, and could trace him too,' says Demetrius"[2] (*Poetaster*, V. 1).

Demetrius is certainly Dekker, and, except the statement just quoted, has nothing whatever in common with Anaides and Carlo, who are just as certainly Marston. We may explain the identity of the charges brought against Crites and Horace by Anaides and Demetrius as being due to the instigation of the original of Anaides (Marston), who, in the passage under consideration, is represented as deliberately getting others, Hedon in this case, to spread this accusation. Demetrius (Dekker) who was "hired" to abuse Horace, simply repeated a charge which had become a common means of annoying Jonson. The reply of Crites to the suggestion of Anaides, which was overheard, "Do good Detraction do," is perhaps a reference to Marston's dedication of *The Scourge*

---

[1] III. 2. Perhaps the statement recorded by Drummond may have been inspired by a similar charge made against Jonson: "Marston wrott his Father-in-lawes preachings, and his Father-in-law his Commedies." *Jonson's Conversations with Drummond*, p. 16. Marston married a daughter of William Wilkes, chaplain to James I.

[2] *Chronicle of the English Drama*, I. 364. On p. 365 Anaides is again identified with Dekker.

of Villanie "To his most esteemed and best beloved Self." The opening poem is headed, "To Detraction I present my Poesie." In the same speech (III. 2) in which Crites calls Anaides "Detraction," we find Hedon and Anaides described respectively as —

> The one a light voluptuous reveller,
> The other, a strange arrogating puff,
> Both impudent and ignorant enough.

Dekker quotes these lines in *Satiromastix*[1] as if they referred to Crispinus (Marston) and Demetrius (Dekker). As no attack on Dekker had been made in *Cynthia's Revels*, he appropriated to himself lines which referred to another of Jonson's enemies.

The mistress of Anaides is Moria, a relationship which indicates Jonson's opinion of Marston. In the scene (IV. 1) in which the four mistresses talk over the merits of the four gallants, Anaides is criticised for having a voice "like the opening of some justice's gate, or a post-boy's horn"; his face is "like a sea-monster," but his worst fault seems to be that "he puts off the calves of his legs, with his stockings every night." This is another allusion to Marston's small legs, the sign of gentle birth. In the game "substantives and adjectives" (IV. 1), Anaides gives as his adjective "white-livered," and explains, "white-livered breeches" by —

> Why! are not their linings white? besides, when they come in swaggering company, and will pocket up anything, may they not properly be said to be white-livered?

The unusual adjective is entirely in keeping with the general style of Marston's vocabulary. Amorphus and Anaides quarrel (IV. 1), as Puntarvolo and Carlo did in *Every Man out of his Humour*, and Anaides goes out with the characteristic language,

---

[1] *The Dramatic Works of Dekker*, I. 195.

"I will garter my hose with your guts." The last word seems to have been a favorite with Marston, if we may judge from his frequent use of it in his works.

Anaides boasts (IV. 1) that he has "put down" Crites "a thousand times" and yet "never talked with him but twice."

> I could never get him to argue with me but once; and then because I could not construe an author I quoted at first sight, he went away and laughed at me.

This may refer to some actual incident, for we know of Jonson's pedantry, and of his contempt for all who were not familiar with the classics. Anaides tells Amorphus (V. 2) to "disgrace this fellow [Crites] in the black stuff." "He is a scholar besides. You may disgrace him here with authority." As Amorphus is Anthony Monday, probably at this time pageant-poet,[1] there may be some significance in the fact that Anaides tries to get him to disgrace Crites. Throughout the play the sole object of Anaides is to injure Crites. In the character we have Jonson's second representation of Marston. This is proved by the close resemblance of Anaides to Carlo Buffone, and by the fact that in *Satiromastix* Dekker quotes, as referring to Crispinus (Marston), lines in *Cynthia's Revels* which refer to Anaides.

In Hedon we have Jonson's third representation of Daniel, who appeared in the previous plays as Master Mathew and Fastidious Brisk. Hedon is "a gallant wholly consecrated to his pleasures," as may be inferred also from the name of his mistress, Madam Philautia.

> He doth ... keep a barber and a monkey; he has a rich wrought waistcoat to entertain his visitants in, with a cap almost suitable. His curtains and bedding are thought to be his own: his bathing-tub is not suspected. He loves to have a fencer, a pedant, and a musician seen in his lodging a-mornings. ... Himself is a rhymer, and that's thought better

---

[1] See above, p. 38.

than a poet. . . . He is thought a very necessary perfume for the presence, and for that only cause welcome thither : six milliner's shops afford you not the like scent. He courts ladies with how many great horse he hath rid that morning, or how oft he hath done the whole or half the pommado in a seven-night before.[1]

The last statement reminds us of the boasts of Fastidious Brisk about his horses and riding.[2]

Jonson seems never to have lost an opportunity to attack Daniel, and in the *Epistle to Elizabeth, Countess of Rutland*, refers to him as a "verser," or "poet, in the court account." He told Drummond that Daniel was "no poet."[3] When Hedon and Anaides appear (II. 1), Hedon is rejoicing because he has invented two new "courtier-like" oaths, "By the tip of your ear, sweet lady" and "By the white valley that lies between the alpine hills of your bosom." He is devoted to Philautia, whom he calls his "Honour," while she styles him her "Ambition" (IV. 1).[4] Of course the ambition of Philautia (self-love) is Hedon (pleasure). There is much of this play upon the meanings of the names of the characters. Daniel was on terms of intimacy with many noble ladies, a fact which was alluded to in treating of Fastidious Brisk,[5] and it is perhaps in allusion to Daniel's verses to ladies that Asotus says (III. 1) that he has " heard Hedon spoke to for some" (verses).

---

[1] II. 1.

[2] *Every Man out of his Humour*, II. 1. In the "Character," prefixed to the play, it is said that Fastidious Brisk "will borrow another man's horse to praise, and backs him as his own."

[3] *Jonson's Conversations with Drummond*, p. 2.

[4] "Ambition" and "Honour" may perhaps be allusions, the force of which is lost upon us, to several uses of the words in the sonnets to Delia; such as "ambition-reared walls," Sonnet XLII.; "ambitious thoughts," Sonnet XII.; "unambitious muse," Sonnet LV.; "honour" is used in Sonnets XIX., L., and LV. There may be some hidden significance in the word "barbarous," given by Hedon in the game "substantives and adjectives" (IV. 1). Daniel uses the word in Sonnet XLII., "barb'rous hand."

[5] See above, p. 54.

Philautia says (IV. 1), "I should be some Laura or some Delia." Mr. Fleay has noticed [1] this evident allusion to Sonnet XLIII.[2] to Delia, in which Daniel says of Delia —

> Though thou, a Laura, hast no Petrarch found,

and also in the same sonnet —

> For though that Laura better limned be.

Delia is referred to again when Crites says to Hedon (V. 2) : —

Nay, stay, my dear Ambition. I can do you over too. You that tell your mistress, her beauty is all composed of theft ; her hair stole from Apollo's goldy-locks ; her white and red, lilies and roses stolen out of Paradise : her eyes two stars, plucked from the sky ; her nose the gnomon of Love's dial, that tells you how the clock of your heart goes ; and for her other parts, as you cannot reckon them, they are so many ; so you cannot recount them, they are so manifest.[3]

Sonnet XIX. to Delia is as follows : —

> Restore thy tresses to the golden Ore,
> Yeeld Cithereas sonne those Arkes of love ;
> Bequeath the heavens the starres that I adore,
> And to th' Orient do thy Pearles remove,
> Yeeld thy hands pride unto th' Ivory white,
> T' Arabian odors give thy breathing sweete :
> Restore thy blush unto Aurora bright,
> To Thetis give the honour of thy feete.
> Let Venus have thy graces, her resign'd,
> And thy sweet voice give back unto the Spheares :
> But yet restore thy fierce and cruell mind,
> To Hyrcan Tygres, and to ruthles Beares.
> Yeeld to the Marble thy hard hart againe :
> So shalt thou cease to plague, and I to paine.[4]

---

[1] *Chronicle of the English Drama*, I. 96.   [2] *Daniel*, ed. Grosart, I. 65.

[3] Perhaps the point of the criticism is that the beauties are stolen. Jonson accused Daniel of plagiarism when he drew the character of Master Mathew, who uttered "nothing but stolen remnants" (see above, p. 27). The whole passage is a criticism on Italianate poetry, in which such comparisons were common, and lines almost precisely similar to the sonnet of Daniel might be cited from the works of other authors of the time.   [4] *Daniel*, ed. Grosart, I. 49.

Daniel's position as a court poet is alluded to (III. 1) when Asotus says to Amorphus, who was instructing him in court ways, " How if they would have me to make verses? I heard Hedon spoke to for some."

Hedon sings to his mistress (IV. 1) a song entitled " The Kiss," and says : " I made this ditty and the note to it, upon a kiss that my Honour gave me." Amorphus criticises the song, and speaks of the " long die-note " as being "too long." One of the constant boasts of Fastidious Brisk is that he had kissed the hand of a countess. When Hedon speaks a few words of Italian (V. 2), we have perhaps an allusion to the fact that both Hedon (Daniel) and Amorphus (Monday) had traveled in Italy.[1] In III. 2, Anaides addresses Hedon as " my dear Envy." *Poetaster* opens with Envy arising in the middle of the stage and making a speech against the author. These two facts have been connected, and it has been thought that perhaps Daniel was meant by the Envy Prologue to *Poetaster*.[2]

---

[1] Sonnet LII. to Delia is entitled " At the Author's Going into Italy," *Daniel*, ed. Grosart, I. 71. Monday has left an account of his travels in Italy in his *English Romayne Life* (1582).

[2] There can be no reasonable doubt that Daniel was the man represented in the character of Hedon. There are, however, critics who hold a different opinion concerning Hedon. Mr. C. H. Herford says: " It can hardly be doubted that Hedon, 'the light voluptuous reveller' in *Cynthia's Revels*, is Marston, but the character, like that of his companion, Anaides, is to our eyes kept studiously within the limits of the abstract and typical satire by which no man's withers are wrung. The portrait was, nevertheless, sufficiently accurate to be fiercely resented, and Marston and his crew prepared an elaborate revenge." *Ben Jonson*, ed. Brinsley Nicholson, Mermaid Series, Introductory Essay by C. H. Herford, p. xxix. No comment is necessary, for we have shown that Anaides is Marston and Hedon is Daniel. It seems somewhat of a contradiction when a critic describes a character as " abstract and typical satire by which no man's withers are wrung," and proceeds in the next sentence to say that the character was " sufficiently accurate to be fiercely resented." Jonson's characters, when satirical, are both concrete and personal, as is shown by the antagonism which they excited. Mr. Herford makes the following statement, which seems at variance with his opinions quoted above : " Of his enmities *The Poetaster* remained, so far as we have certain evidence, the last, as it was the first, direct dramatic expression" (*ibid*., p. liii). The common mis-

Asotus is described by Hedon (IV. 1) as "some idle Fungoso that hath got above the cupboard since yesterday." This identifies Asotus with Fungoso in *Every Man out of his Humour* and therefore with Lodge.[1] Asotus is described in the Induction as —

a citizen's heir, Asotus, or the Prodigal, who, in imitation of the traveller [Amorphus], who hath the Whetstone [Cos] following him, entertains the Beggar [Prosaites], to be his attendant.

Amorphus, when about to meet Asotus, is in doubt how to address him, whether

to talk of some hospital whose walls record his father a benefactor? or of so many buckets bestowed on his parish church in his life time, with his name at length, for want of arms, trickt upon them? any of these. Or to praise the cleanness of the street wherein he dwelt? or the provident painting of his posts, against he should have been prætor? or leaving his parent, come to some special ornament about himself, as his rapier, or some other of his accoutrements?[2]

These references to the father of Asotus agree substantially with the facts concerning Sir Thomas Lodge, the father of the poet. Sir Thomas Lodge was a wealthy grocer who was alderman of Cheap Ward in 1553, sheriff in 1556, and Lord Mayor of London in 1563, — a fact to which Jonson alludes, when he tells us that Philargyrus, the father of Asotus, "was to have been prætor next year." He left in his

---

take concerning Dekker is made by Mr. Herford when he says: "It is certain that both Dekker and Marston were portrayed in the Hedon and Anaides of *Cynthia's Revels.*" *The Dictionary of National Biography*, XXX. 182. Dr. Cartwright identifies Hedon with Marston and Anaides with Dekker, *Shakespeare and Jonson, Dramatic versus Wit Combats*, p. 17. Simpson states that *Cynthia's Revels* was "written against Marston and Dekker, who figure in it as Hedon and Anaides." *The School of Shakspere*, II. 129. Mr. Bullen says "It is certain that [in the characters of Anaides and Hedon] Jonson was glancing particularly at Marston and Dekker." *Marston*, I. p. xxxiii.

[1] See above, p. 56, for the identification of Fungoso with Lodge.
[2] I. 1.

will five pounds for the poor in Westham, Essex.[1] The "painting of his posts" has reference to the fact that Lodge's father was sheriff.[2] The passage in which Asotus is described by Mercury contains the description of Amorphus also. As they are closely associated, the whole passage is given here. Mercury says : —

A notable smelt. One that hath newly entertained the beggar [Prosaites] to follow him, but cannot get him to wait near enough. 'T is Asotus, the heir of Philargyrus ; but first I 'll give ye the other's character, which may make his the clearer. He that is with him is Amorphus, a traveller, one so made out of the mixture of shreds of forms that himself is truly deformed. He walks most commonly with a clove or pick-tooth in his mouth, he is the very mint of compliment, all his behaviours are printed, his face is another volume of essays, and his beard is an Aristarchus. He speaks all cream skimmed, and more affected than a dozen waiting-women. He is his own promoter in every place. The wife of the ordinary gives him his diet to maintain her table in discourse ; which indeed is a mere tyranny over her other guests, for he will usurp all the talk : ten constables are not so tedious. He is no great shifter : once a year his apparel is ready to revolt. He doth use much to arbitrate quarrels, and fights himself, exceeding well, out at a window. He will lie cheaper than any beggar, and louder than most clocks : for which he is right properly accommodated to the Whetstone, his page. The other gallant is his zany, and doth most of these tricks after him ; sweats to imitate him in everything to a hair, except a beard, which is not yet extant. He doth learn to make strange sauces, to eat anchovies, maccaroni, bovoli, fagioli, and caviare, because he loves them ; speaks as he speaks, looks, walks, goes so in clothes and fashion ; is in all as if he were moulded of him. Marry, before they met, he had other very pretty sufficiencies, which yet he retains some light impression of ; as frequenting a dancing school, and grievously torturing strangers with inquisition after his grace in his galliard. He buys a fresh acquaintance at any rate. His eyes and his raiment confer much together as he goes in the

---

[1] The facts concerning Sir Thomas Lodge are given by Mr. Charles Welch in *The Dictionary of National Biography*, XXXIV. 59.

[2] At the door of the sheriff's house were posts on which proclamations were "posted." In *Twelfth Night* (I. 5) Malvolio says of Viola, "he 'll stand at your door like a sheriff's post."

street. He treads nicely, like the fellow that walks upon ropes, especially the first Sunday of his silk stockings ; and when he is most neat and new, you shall strip him with commendations.[1]

The tailor's bill, which was made so prominent in the career of Fungoso[2] is not referred to in connection with Asotus, unless, indeed, it is glanced at in several passages, as when Asotus is said (IV. 1) to " look like a tailor . . . that hath sayed on one of his customer's suits."

In the relations of Argurion to Asotus we have a delightfully satirical account of the fortunes of Lodge, whose father was a very wealthy man,[3] — a fact which makes significant the name assigned him, Philargyrus, and also the advice given to Asotus by Amorphus : —

> That was your father's love, the nymph Argurion. I would have you direct all your courtship thither ; if you could but endear yourself to her affection, you were eternally engallanted.[4]

It is quite evident from this that Lodge was not rich, a fact which we know from other sources, for his father makes no mention of his son Thomas in his will, and the poet speaks of himself as " poor to the world."[5] Argurion is enamoured of Asotus, and gives him jewels (IV. 1) which he afterwards gives to Hedon. When Argurion sees that Asotus is false to her (IV. 1) she faints, and is carried out by Morus and Asotus,

---

[1] II. 1. The description of Asotus is in accord with the characterization of Lodge by Gosson, who speaks of " one in wit simple ; in learning ignorant ; in attempt rash ; in name Lodge." *Plays Confuted in Five Actions.*

[2] See above, p. 56.

[3] Sir Thomas Lodge, in 1553. received a sum of £15,426, paid to him and other merchants in consideration of money advanced by them to the Queen (*State Papers, For. Ser.,* 1553-58, p. 30). He became surety for redeeming Sir Henry Palmer, prisoner in France, and seems to have been able by his wealth to aid the Queen in many ways.

[4] IV. 1.

[5] *Phillis Honoured with Pastoral Sonnets,* Sonnet XL., Hunterian Club Reprint, p. 57.

while Mercury remarks: "Well, I doubt all the physic he has will scarce recover her; she's too far spent." The play on the word "Argurion" is clear. We have here another allusion to the career of Lodge, who, after engaging in various pursuits, began the study of medicine in 1596, and was granted the degree Doctor of Physic, at Avignon, in 1600.[1] Lodge's later books bear on the title-page his name, with the title, "Doctor of Physic." The remark of Mercury means that Lodge's knowledge of medicine will never bring him money. Two more descriptions of Asotus are given. One by Argurion (IV. 1) represents him as "a most delicate youth; a sweet face, a straight body, a well-proportioned leg and foot, a white hand, a tender voice." To this Philautia and Phantaste add comments concerning his nose, hair, and eyes, and say that "he would have made a most neat barber-surgeon." The other description is where Crites, after the absurd challenge has been issued by Amorphus and Asotus (V. 2) says to Mercury:—

> Sir, this [Asotus] is the wight of worth that dares you to the encounter. A gentleman of so pleasing and ridiculous a carriage; as even standing, carries meat in the mouth, you see; and, I assure you, although no bred courtling, yet a most particular man, of goodly havings, well fashioned 'haviour, and of as hardened and excellent a bark as the most naturally qualified amongst them, informed, reformed, and transformed from his original citycism.

In the challenge (V. 2) Asotus is called Acolastus Polypragmon[2] Asotus (Unwhipped[3] Jack-of-all-trades Prodigal), a name peculiarly fittting to Lodge, whose various professions have been alluded to. We do not know the cause of Jonson's hostility to Lodge. It seems that Jonson intended to make the

---

[1] See Mr. Sidney Lee's account of Lodge's life in *The Dictionary of National Biography*, XXXIV. 60.

[2] πολυπράγμων generally means "a busybody." The translation "Jack-of-all-trades" seems more appropriate here.

[3] cf. Shakespeare's use of the word "unwhipped." *Lear*, III. 2, 53.

identification of Asotus certain, for when Phantaste calls Asotus "our gold-finch," we have probably an allusion to the name "Golde," by which Lodge anagrammatically calls himself in a pastoral dialogue addressed to Rowland (Drayton) in *A Fig for Momus*, 1595.[1]

"This silent gentleman," Asotus (IV. 1), is the same as Fungoso, "Kinsman to Justice Silence," in *Every Man out of his Humour* (V. 2).[2] When Asotus says (V. 2) —

> As buckets are put down into a well,
> Or as a schoolboy . . .

he is interrupted by Crites with the exclamation —

> Truss up your simile, Jackaw!

The editors of Jonson have not noted that this is a criticism of an epigram by Sir John Davies.[3]

Asotus is brother of the citizen's wife (V. 2). The citizen and his wife are the same persons as Deliro and Fallace in *Every Man out of his Humour*, and as Albius and Chloe in *Poetaster*. Fungoso is brother of Fallace.

The character of Amorphus as described by Mercury has been quoted above. We learn further concerning him, that he is a great traveller, and has been to Italy; speaks Spanish and Italian (I. 1). Amorphus says of himself : —

---

[1] *A Fig for Momus*, Eclogue 3, Hunterian Club Reprint, p. 23.
[2] *Chronicle of the English Drama*, Fleay, I. 364.

> XXIX. *In Haywodum.*
> Haywood which did in epigrams excell
> Is now put down since my light muse arose,
> As buckets are put down into a well,
> Or as a schoolboy putteth down his hose.
>
> *Sir John Davies.* ed. Grosart, II. 29.

This epigram is thus alluded to by Sir John Harington in *Metamorphosis of Ajax*, 1596 : "Haywood for his proverbs and epigrams is not yet put down by any of our country, though one doth indeed come near him, that graces him the more in saying he puts him down."

But, knowing myself an essence so sublimated and refined by travel; of so studied and well-exercised a gesture; so alone in fashion; able to render the face of any statesman living:[1] and to speak the mere extraction of language; one that hath now made the sixth return upon venture;[2] and was your first that ever enriched his country with the true laws of the duello;[3] whose optics have drunk the spirit of beauty in some eightscore and eighteen princes' courts where I have resided, and been there fortunate in the amours of three hundred forty and five ladies, all nobly, if not princely, descended; whose names I have in catalogue.

Amorphus is fond of using foreign phrases and of boasting of his travels. He is the teacher of Asotus in those things that pertain to courtier-like conduct. The absurd language of courtship, which Amorphus teaches Asotus to use (III. 3), is similar to that employed by Puntarvolo in *Every Man out of his Humour* (II. 1). Phantaste says that "the traveller Amorphus"

---

[1] It will be shown that Amorphus is probably Anthony Monday, who was an actor as well as a playwright. It is probable that this passage alludes to the ability of Monday to imitate on the stage the appearance and actions of other people. Amorphus gives an exhibition of his powers of imitation in Act II. Sc. 1. It was a common thing in plays thus to amuse the spectators. Cf. *The Return from Parnassus*, IV. 3, where Kemp gives such an exhibition.

[2] Amorphus is the same man as Puntarvolo in *Every Man out of his Humour*. Cf. Puntarvolo's proposed trip to Constantinople "upon venture."

[3] Mr. Fleay says: "Amorphus, the Deformed Traveller, who 'enriched his country with the true laws of the duello' (I. 1), must have been the translator of Saviolo's *Practise*, S. R. 1594, Nov. 19. I think Barnaby Rich is the man." *Chronicle of the English Drama*, 1. 363. Mr. Fleay is probably right in the first statement. We do not know what reasons he has for the second regarding the identity of the translator. If Saviolo's *Practise* is referred to in the passage under consideration, it is possible that Jonson's play may enable us to determine the identity of the hitherto unknown translator. There is almost conclusive evidence that Amorphus is Anthony Monday, and an examination of the works of Monday, who translated many books from Italian, French, and Spanish, shows that the translation of Saviolo's *Practise* would have been entirely in accord with what we know him to have done. There is no reason for supposing that Jonson had any quarrel with Barnaby Rich, or cause to satirize him, as must have been the case if he is represented as Amorphus. There is no evidence whatever that Barnaby Rich translated Saviolo. No translator is named on the title-page of Saviolo's *Practise*, printed by John Wolfe, London, 1595, quarto.

is the "properest" of the gallants, and Philautia says that he "looks like a Venetian trumpeter in the battle of Lepanto, in the gallery yonder; and speaks to the tune of a country lady, that comes ever in the rearward or train of a fashion." When Mercury says (II. 1), "Amorphus, a traveller, one so made out of the mixture of shreds of forms, that himself is truly deformed," the interpretation may be found, perhaps, in the following statement of Antonio Balladino (Anthony Monday): "Why, I'll tell you, Master Onion, I do use as much stale stuff, though I say it myself, as any man does in that kind, I am sure. Did you see the last pageant I set forth?"[1]

In the game "substantives and adjectives" (IV. 1), the adjective suggested by Amorphus is "pythagorical," which is one of the "fustian" words ridiculed by Clove in *Every Man out of his Humour* (III. 1).[2] Marston is not the only writer whose vocabulary is ridiculed by Jonson, for, as has been shown, some of the "fustian" not found in Marston's works is put into the mouth of Brisk and Puntarvolo. Amorphus, like Puntarvolo,[3] uses "optic" (I. 1), a "fustian" word of Clove's. Of the words disgorged by Crispinus (*Poetaster*, V. 1) Amorphus uses "retrograde" (V. 2) and Crites uses "reciprocal" (I. 1).[4] The language of Amorphus is ridiculed in many passages, and when his use of "ingenious," "acute," and "polite" is ridiculed, Hedon says (IV. 1) that Amorphus "cannot speak out of a dictionary method." The word "arride," used by Amorphus (III. 3; IV. 1), is ridiculed when used by Fastidious Brisk.[5] Amorphus uses "intrinsecate" (V. 2), one of the "new-minted epithets" attacked by Marston in *The Scourge of Villanie*.[6]

---

[1] *The Case is Altered*, I. 1.
[2] See above, p. 51.
[3] *Every Man out of his Humour*, II. 1.
[4] Amorphus uses "reciprocally," IV. 1.
[5] *Every Man out of his Humour*, II. 1.
[6] See above, p. 5.

The facts concerning Amorphus agree in many particulars with what we know about Anthony Monday, who was attacked by Jonson as Antonio Balladino in *The Case is Altered*,[1] and as Puntarvolo in *Every Man out of his Humour*. The proof of the latter identification is largely dependent on the evident identity of Puntarvolo and Amorphus.[2] Amorphus boasts of his travels, and of the distinguished people he has met. He has been to Italy and France, and has a knowledge of various languages.[3] Anthony Monday went to Rome in 1578, impelled to travel, as he tells us, by "a desire to see strange countries, and also affection to learn the languages."[4] He was one of the messengers of Her Majesty's Chamber about 1584, and it seems probable that he went with Pembroke's company on their foreign tour in 1598.[5]

Amorphus says to Asotus (II. 1), "You shall now as well be the ocular as the ear-witness, how clearly I can refel that paradox, or rather pseudodox, of those which hold the face to be the index of the mind." Anthony Monday translated from the French a book which he entitled *The Defence of Contraries. Paradoxes against common opinion, debated in Forme of Declamations in Place of public Censure: onlie to exercise young wittes*

---

[1] See above, p. 37.
[2] See above, p. 64.
[3] For similar facts concerning Puntarvolo, see above, p. 64.
[4] *The English Romayne Life*, by Anthony Monday (1582 and 1590, quarto), reprinted in *The Harleian Miscellany*, VII. 129. This book gives an account of the life of Englishmen at the seminary in Rome at which Monday was entertained. He travelled with Thomas Nowell, and on the way from Boulogne to Amiens fell into the hands of marauding soldiers. He proceeded to Paris, where the English ambassador gave him money to enable him to return to London, but instead of doing so he went to Rome, stopping on his way at Lyons, Milan, Bologna, Florence, and Vienna. See account of Monday by Mr. Thomas Seccombe in *The Dictionary of National Biography*, XXXIX. 290.
[5] See above, p. 42, note. Cf. also the proposed travels of Puntarvolo in *Every Man out of his Humour*.

in difficult matters.¹ There is, perhaps, in the words of Amorphus, an allusion to this book. Amorphus is constantly referred to as "the traveller," a title which Monday deserved on account of his actual travels. Jonson attacks not only Monday, but also his writings. Webbe, in his *Discourse of English Poetrie*, 1586, speaks of Monday as "an earnest traveller in this art [*i.e.*, poetry]."² It is possible that Jonson had in mind Webbe's criticism, and in calling Amorphus a "traveller," used the word in a double sense.

Hedon's poem, "The Kiss," is criticised by Amorphus, who thinks the "die-note" too long, and who, after a lengthy explanation, sings some verses (IV. 1) on a glove which "the beauteous lady Annabel" gave him. He explains that he had set the words to his "most affected instrument, the lyra." After singing, he calls attention to the care that he had taken in fitting words to music:—

Do you not observe how excellently the ditty is affected in every place? that I do not marry a word of short quantity to a long note? nor an ascending syllable to a descending tone? Besides, upon the word "best"³ there, you see how I do enter with an odd minum, and drive it through the brief: which no intelligent musician, I know, but will affirm to be very rare, extraordinary and pleasing.

---

¹ The title-page (see Lowndes' *Bibliographers' Manual*, 1630, III.) states that the book was "translated out of French by A. M., Messenger of Her Majesty's Chamber." Halliwell, contrary to the evidence furnished by the title-page, attributed the book to Lodge. The book was published in 1593.
² *A Discourse of English Poetrie*, by William Webbe, reprint by Arber, p. 35.
³ Referring to the last line of the song:—
That was thy mistress *best* of gloves.
Jonson in this song ridicules the affected language of the courtiers. The first line of the poem on the glove is "Thou *more than most sweet* glove." In *Every Man out of his Humour* (V. 1) Macilente tells Sogliardo, "Be sure to kiss your hand often enough; pray for her health, and tell her how *more than most fair* she is." Amorphus tells Asotus (III. 3) to take his mistress by the "rosy-fingered hand," and "then offering to kiss her hand, if she shall coyly recoil, and signify your repulse: you are to reënforce yourself with *more than most fair* lady." See above, p. 25, note.

Amorphus wrote only the words of the song. Anthony Monday wrote a number of songs which he set to tunes by various composers. In 1588 he published a book entitled *A Banquet of Daintie Conceits; furnished with verie delicate and choyce Inventions to delight their mindes who take Pleasure in Musique: and therewithal to sing sweete Ditties either to the Lute, Bandora, Virginalles, or anie other Instrument.* The hostility of Amorphus to Anaides (whom he terms [IV. 1] "rude, debauched, impudent, coarse, unpolished, a frapler and base") is in accord with what we have learned of the relations between Monday and Marston. Evidence has been adduced to prove that in *Histriomastix* Marston satirized Monday as Posthast.[1] There was evidently a quarrel between the two men, a fact which Jonson did not fail to use in *Cynthia's Revels* as he had used it in *Every Man out of his Humour*, in which (V. 4) Puntarvolo (Monday) finally sealed up Carlo's (Marston's) mouth.

There are yet other facts which tend to prove the identity of Amorphus and Anthony Monday.[2] In 1598 Jonson satirized Monday as Antonio Balladino, "pageant-poet to the city of Milan."[3] He is said to lack originality, and to be unable to

---

[1] See above, p. 41.

[2] Attempts to identify Amorphus have led to some interesting conclusions. A writer (qy. Simpson?) in *The North British Review* (1870, p. 407) says of "Amorphus, the Deformed": "There are indications that Shakespeare had been already nicknamed 'Deformed' by the purist school of critics, who, ever since Nash in 1589, and Greene in 1592, had been attacking him for ignorance of art, for decking himself in other men's feathers, and gleaning his wit at second hand. This supposition gives a very piquant meaning to the joke in *Much Ado about Nothing*, about 'one Deformed,' whom Dogberry and his wise watchman had known as a 'vile thief this seven year.'" Simpson, in a paper on *The Political use of the Stage* (Transactions of the New Shakspere Society, 1874, Part II. p. 391) says: "In *Cynthia's Revels*, 'Amorphus, or the Deformed,' evidently represents the person mentioned in *Much Ado*, as 'one Deformed,' 'a vile thief this seven year.'" Mr. Fleay identifies "one Deformed" in *Much Ado* with Nashe, but not with Amorphus. *Chronicle of the English Drama*, II. 144.

[3] *The Case is Altered*, I. 1.

invent anything new for his pageants. Monday was for many years pageant-poet to the city of London.[1] The second game played by the gallants and their mistresses (IV. 1) results in the following statement : —

> An oration was made by a traveller, with a glyster, in a pair of pained slops, last progress for the delight of ladies. A few heat drops and a month's mirth followed, and this silent gentleman (Asotus) would have done it better.

The "traveller" here, as elsewhere in the play, is Amorphus (Monday), and the allusion is to a pageant set forth at the "last progress."[2] Toward the close of the same almost interminable scene (IV. 1) it is announced that Cynthia intends to appear, and Amorphus at once suggests presenting a masque.

> *Amorphus.* What say you to a masque?
> *Hedon.* Nothing better, if the project were new and rare.
> *Arete.* Why, I'll send for Crites, and have his advice : be you ready in your endeavours : he shall discharge you of the inventive part.

Amorphus resents the suggestion that Crites (Jonson) be asked to assist in the preparation of the masque, and with an injured and indignant air asks, "Have not I invention afore him? learning to better that invention above him? and infanted with pleasant travel?"

At the opening of the last act, Crites is told by Mercury that the purpose of the night's entertainment is to rebuke the courtiers for their follies. In the next scene (V. 2), Arete, ignoring entirely Amorphus, who had made the suggestion, tells Crites to prepare a masque. In the circumstances just mentioned, Jonson reiterates the old charge, made in *The Case is Altered*, that Monday had no powers of invention, and was unfit to be pageant-poet. The only suitable person for the

---

[1] See above, p. 38.
[2] The second game, "A thing done and who did it," was printed first in the folio 1616. As we do not know the date at which it was written we cannot tell to what pageant or progress reference is here made.

office was Crites (Jonson). We have here, probably, the reason for Jonson's repeated satire of Monday. We have suggested that Jonson's hostility to Daniel was for a similar reason,[1] for Daniel had, through court influence, obtained the position of poet-laureate, a position coveted by Jonson. In the Palinode, Amorphus craves pardon, among other things, for "squiring to tilt-yards, play-houses, pageants, and all such public places."

After what has been said of the other characters, and incidentally, of their relations to Crites, there is need to add but little concerning him. Jonson draws his own picture, emphasizing his virtues and praising himself without stint. It is Crites alone that Arete praises, and he alone is welcome at the court of Cynthia. The most significant scene is perhaps that (III. 2) in which Anaides and Hedon plot against Crites, who does not deign to notice them. The chief charges brought against him in the play are his wearing of shabby clothes and his being a scholar (III. 2). Jonson's failure to gain money by his works is represented in the unsuccessful attempt (IV. 1) to make Argurion bestow favor on Crites. The speeches of Crites are characteristic criticism of the follies of the time. It is contrary to our ideas for a man to describe himself as "a creature of a most perfect and divine temper : one in whom the humours and elements are peaceably met, etc.," and when Jonson so described himself as Crites, it is not surprising that he aroused antagonism. He denied the existence in himself of those vices and follies with which he was only too ready to charge other men.

Of his accusers, he says (III. 2):

<pre>
             So they be ill men
    If they spake worse, 'twere better.
      .   .   .   .
         .   .   . but when I remember
    'T is Hedon and Anaides, alas, then
      I think but what they are, and am not stirred.
</pre>

---

[1] See above, p. 13.

In several passages Crites describes his four foes, and after one such passage (V. 2) Mercury says: "Sir, you have played the painter yourself, and limned them to the life." It is this passage that Marston had in mind when he introduced the painter with two pictures in *Antonio and Mellida*.[1] At the conclusion of the masques (V. 3), the courtiers, who had gained access to Cynthia's presence by pretending to be what they were not, are sentenced by Crites to sing the Palinode, in which are set forth the faults and follies of courtiers in general, but especially of the four men satirized in the play. The Epilogue, in Jonson's most characteristic vein, ends with the line so often quoted by his enemies: —

    By —— 'tis good, and if you like 't, you may.

---

[1] This scene is discussed below.

VII.

ANTONIO AND MELLIDA AND THE SPANISH TRAGEDY.

THE *History of Antonio and Mellida* and *Antonio's Revenge* were both performed in 1600, and published, quarto, in 1602. They are the last plays of Marston's from which words and phrases are ridiculed in *Poetaster* (1601). This ridicule connects *Antonio's Revenge* with "The War of the Theatres." *Antonio and Mellida* enters into our discussion, not only because Jonson ridiculed the vocabulary employed in it, but also because there is undoubtedly a close connection between the scene (V. 1) in which a painter is asked to paint "Uh!" and to "make a picture sing," and a scene, probably written by Jonson, in *The Spanish Tragedy* (IV.), in which Hieronimo requests Bazardo to paint "a doleful cry."

In *Cynthia's Revels* (V. 2) Mercury, replying to the description of the characters by Crites, says :—

> Sir, you have played the painter yourself, and limned them to the life.

In *Antonio and Mellida* (V. 1) Balurdo says to the painter, who states that he "did limn" the two pictures which he brought :

> Limn them? a good word, limn them: whose picture is this? *Anno Domini*, 1599. Believe me, Master *Anno Domini* was of a good settled age when you limned him: 1599 years old! Let's see the other. *Aetatis suae* 24. Byrlady, he is somewhat younger. Belike Master *Aetatis Suae* was *Anno Domini's* son.

Marston's ridicule of Jonson's word "limn" is plain, and the two pictures are probably the two representations of Marston, the first as Carlo Buffone in *Every Man out of his Humour* in 1599, the second as Anaides in *Cynthia's Revels* in 1600. Twenty-four years, the age of *Aetatis Suae*, was almost certainly the age of Marston in 1600,[1] when Jonson represented him as Anaides.

It has been thought by some critics[2] that the great similarity between the painter scene (V. 1) in *Antonio and Mellida* and the scene in *The Spanish Tragedy* (IV.) is the result of an attempt by Marston to parody a scene written by Jonson. There is no positive proof that Jonson wrote the Painter scene in *The Spanish Tragedy*, although it is probable that he did, for we know that in 1601 and 1602 he wrote additions to a play which Henslowe called *Geronymo*,[3] but which was, as Collier has pointed out, almost certainly *The Spanish Tragedy*.[4] That the painter scene was one of the "adicyons" mentioned by

---

[1] On Feb. 4, 1591-92, "John Marston, aged 16, a gentleman's son, of co. Warwick," was matriculated at Brazennose College, Oxford. (See Dr. Grosart's Introduction to *Marston's Poems*, p. x, quoted by Mr. Bullen, *The Works of John Marston*, I. xii.) That this John Marston was the poet is all but certain. His age was twenty-four or twenty-five years in 1600.

[2] Mr. Fleay says: "Jonson, early in 1600, in *Cynthia's Revels* (V. 2), 'played the painter, and limned to the life' Anaides, Hedon, and Amorphus. . . . He also wrote the additional scene with the painter in it in Kyd's *Spanish Tragedy*, which was, perhaps, acted by the Chapel children 1599-1600 (see Induction to *Cynthia's Revels*), wherein Jeronymo requires 'a doleful cry' to be painted. Marston hits both these by introducing a painter who, in 1599, had 'limned' one picture, and in 1600 had represented Marston at twenty-four years old in the other." *Chronicle of the English Drama*, II. 75.

[3] "Lent unto Mr. Alleyn, the 25 of Septembr 1601, to lend unto Bengemen Johnson, upon his writtinge of his adicions in Geronymo, the some of xxxxs." *Henslowe's Diary*, p. 201.

"Lent unto bengemy Johnsone, at the apoyntment of E. Alleyn and Wm. Birde, the 24 of June 1602, in earneste of a boocke called Richard crockbacke, and for new adicyons for Jeronymo, the some of x li." *Ibid.*, p. 223.

[4] *Henslowe's Diary*, ed. Collier, p. 201, note 2. *The Spanish Tragedy* was a second part of the old play *Jeronymo*, to which there is no evidence that additions were ever made. In the Induction to *Cynthia's Revels* (1600) it is said, "Another . . . swears . . . that the old Hieronimo, as it was first acted, was the only best and judiciously penned play of Europe."

Henslowe, seems probable from the evidence furnished by the title-page of the quarto published in 1602.[1] *The Spanish Tragedie: . . . enlarged with new additions of the Painters part and others, as it hath of late been divers times acted. Imprinted at London by W. W. for T. Pavier. . . .* 1602.[2] Since the evidence seems to show that the scene in *The Spanish Tragedy* was written later than the similar scene in *Antonio and Mellida*, and since the similarity of the two scenes is such as almost to exclude even the possibility of their having been written independently of each other, we have left to us three hypotheses on which to explain the relationship of the scenes. If, as seems probable, the scene in *The Spanish Tragedy* was written in 1602, then Marston's scene, if a parody, must have been written later than the rest of *Antonio and Mellida* (1600), and inserted in the play when it was published in 1602. This seems a possible explanation, for Marston's scene is not an organic part of the play, and might have been interpolated. We can find, however, no good reason for any such proceeding on the part of Marston, for, at the late date at which we must necessarily suppose the scene to have been written, his relations with Jonson were probably more amicable than they were in 1600, or at least the "War" was over. Marston had, so far as we know, no reason in 1602 for alluding, as he did so specifically, to *Every Man out of his Humour* and *Cynthia's Revels*, and omitting any reference to the worst and most recent caricature of all, *Poetaster*. A second explanation of the similarity of the two scenes is that given by Mr. Fleay,[3] but, if we accept it, we must ignore the evidence offered by Henslowe's entries, and by the title-page of the 1602 quarto

---

[1] There were earlier quartos of this play in which no mention is made of the painter. See *Dodsley's Old English Plays*, ed. Hazlitt, V. 2; also Halliwell's *Dictionary of Old Plays*.

[2] Title as given in *Dodsley's Old English Plays*, ed. Hazlitt, V. 2.

[3] *Chronicle of the English Drama*, II. 75.

of *The Spanish Tragedy*, and must insist that the painter scene was a part of that play as early as 1599-1600. For the latter supposition there is no evidence. It seems almost certain that Marston did not, in 1600, parody the scene in *The Spanish Tragedy*. A third explanation, and one that is in accord with the evidence, is that Marston's scene was suggested to him by the passage in *Cynthia's Revels*, which had just been performed for the first time, and that the scene in *The Spanish Tragedy* was suggested to Jonson by the scene in *Antonio and Mellida*.

If this last explanation is correct, we find a parallel instance of similarity between a passage by Marston and a passage by Jonson in the speeches of Chrisoganus and Macilente, to which attention has been called.[1]

The Epilogue to *Cynthia's Revels* aroused opposition by its arrogant declaration concerning the play —

By —— 'tis good, and if you like 't you may.

It is to this that the Epilogue to *Antonio and Mellida* evidently refers : —

I stand not as a peremptory challenger of desert, either for him that composed the Comedy, or for us that acted it ; but as a most submissive suppliant for both.

The Epilogue to *Antonio and Mellida* was armed, and Jonson's next play, *Poetaster*, had an armed Prologue.[2]

---

[1] See above, p. 39.
[2] Jonson's armed Prologue was a reply to Marston's armed Epilogue. The Prologue to *Troilus and Cressida* is armed, and speaks lines which may refer to the Prologue to *Poetaster*. The Envy Prologue was an idea borrowed perhaps from *Mucedorus*.

VIII.

POETASTER.

POETASTER is Jonson's only openly avowed reply[1] to attacks made on him by other playwrights. He told Drummond that "he had many quarrells with Marston, beat him, and took his pistol from him, wrote his *Poetaster* on him."[2] The play was first peformed in 1601 by the Chapel children, and was entered S. R. Dec. 21, 1601,[3] and published, quarto, in 1602. The attack on lawyers and soldiers caused Jonson to be brought before the Lord Chief Justice, but his innocence of the charges made against him was answered for by his friend Mr. Richard Martin, to whom he prefixed, in the folio edition[4] of the play (1616), an epistle referring to the incident. Appended to the play in the quarto is this note : —

> Here, reader, in place of the Epilogue was meant to thee an Apology from the Author, with his reasons for the publishing of this book : but, since he is no less restrained, than thou deprived of it by Authority, he prays thee to think charitably of what thou hast read, till thou mayest hear him speak what he hath written.

---

[1] Although Jonson's earlier comedies all contained attacks on other men, yet he never openly acknowledged the fact.

[2] *Jonson's Conversations with Drummond*, p. 20.

[3] *Poetaster* was acted before Dekker's *Satiromastix*, which was in preparation, and which, when it was acted, contained numerous references to *Poetaster*.

[4] The folio (1616) differs in some respects from the quarto (1602). In the third act, the folio contains, as the concluding scene, a dialogue between Horace and Trebatius (a translation of Horace, *Sat.* II. 1) not in the quarto. There are numerous minor differences, mostly verbal, but a very important difference between the two versions is the addition, in the folio, of the "Apologetical Dialogue which was only once spoken upon the stage." This was evidently writ-

Prefixed to the Apologetical Dialogue in the folio is this note : —

TO THE READER.

If, by looking on what is past, thou hast deserved that name, I am willing thou shouldst yet know more, by that which follows, an Apologetical Dialogue ; which was only once spoken upon the stage, and all the answer I ever gave to sundry impotent libels then cast out (and some yet remaining) against me, and this play. Wherein I take no pleasure to revive the times ; but that posterity may make a difference between their manners that provoked me then, and mine that neglected them ever. For, in these strifes, and on such persons, were as wretched to affect a victory, as it is unhappy to be committed with them. *Non annorum canities est laudanda, sed morum.*

In this note, and in the Dialogue which follows, we have a direct mention by Jonson of the stage war in which he had been involved. Nasutus and Polyposus[1] call upon the author at his lodgings to see " how he looks after these libels."[2] The author defends himself, in a manner characteristic of Jonson, by declaring that his play was innocent of offence, " some salt it had, but neither tooth nor gall." He denies having "taxed the law and lawyers, captains and the players by their particular names," and declares that while he attacked vices, he spared persons. He does not know why he has been attacked, but says : —

---

ten after the trouble with the lawyers and soldiers, and also after the acting of *Satiromastix*. It is probable that the " Apology from the Author," from which he was " restrained by authority " in 1602, was made in this " Apologetical Dialogue."

[1] These names are from Martial, 12, 37, and 13, 2. Mr. Fleay suggests that Nasutus may " glance at Ovidius Naso, ' the well-nosed.' " *Chronicle of the English Drama*, I. 369.

[2] " These libels " were probably the legal proceedings against Jonson, as well as criticisms on his play, and possibly Dekker's reply in *Satiromastix*. So far as we can judge, it seems that public opinion was on the side of the lawyers, soldiers, and players whom Jonson had satirized.

> sure I am, three years
> They did provoke me with their petulant styles
> On every stage : and I at last, unwilling,
> But weary, I confess, of so much trouble,
> Thought I would try if shame could win upon 'em ;
> And therefore chose Augustus Cæsar's times,
> When wit and arts were at their height in Rome,
> To shew that Virgil, Horace, and the rest
> Of those great master-spirits, did not want
> Detractors then, or practicers against them.

Jonson remarks successively on his treatment of lawyers, soldiers, and players. He admits that he "brought in Ovid, chid by his angry father for neglecting" the law, but denies any reference to law and lawyers of his own time. "For the captain" he speaks the epigram, "Unto True Soldiers," and against "such as are miscalled captains," referring to Shift, Tucca, and others of that type. He then replies to the charge that he had attacked the players : —

> Now for the players, it is true, I taxed them,
> And yet but some ; and those so sparingly,
> As all the rest might have sat still unquestioned,
> Had they but had the wit or conscience
> To think well of themselves. But, impotent, they
> Thought each man's vice belonged to their whole tribe ;
> And much good do't them ! What they have done 'gainst me,
> I am not moved with : if it gave them meat,
> Or got them clothes, 'tis well ; that was their end.
> Only amongst them, I am sorry for
> Some better natures,[1] by the rest so drawn,
> To run in that vile line.

---

[1] Whalley remarks on the theory of some critics that Shakespeare was one of these "better natures." There is no evidence whatever to substantiate such a theory, but if it could be proved that Shakespeare was involved in "The War of the Theatres," we might possibly find in this passage a reference to the "purge," mentioned in *The Return from Parnassus,* as having been given by Shakespeare to Ben Jonson as a reply to *Poetaster.* The "better natures" were actors and

Polyposus. And is this all!
    Will you not answer, then, the libels!
Author. No.
Polyposus. Nor the Untrussers?[1]
Author. Neither.

An inference drawn from the passage quoted may explain the long duration of "The War of the Theatres." Jonson states here and elsewhere that these satirical plays were profitable to the writers. The plays "gave them meat" and "got them clothes," and this "was their end" in writing them. Histrio says (III. 1) that the reason for hiring Demetrius (Dekker) to bring in Horace (Jonson) and his gallants in a play is that "it will get us a huge deal of money . . . and we have need on't." Of course any profit to be derived from satirical plays could be gained by Jonson as well as by his opponents. Although Jonson was several times involved in legal difficulties on account of his plays,[2] and although the Elizabethan laws concerning libel and slander were severe, and the people of the time were litigious,[3] yet we have no record of

---

playwrights with whom Jonson had no quarrel, but who evidently sympathized with Marston. The reference may be to the Chamberlain's company, by whom *Satiromastix* was performed, or to Dekker who wrote it.

[1] A reference to *Satiromastix*, or, *The Untrussing of the Humorous Poet.*

[2] Once for satirizing lawyers and soldiers in *Poetaster* ; again for his share in *Eastward Ho* (written [1604] with Marston and Chapman) in which allusions to the Scots proved offensive to the King and his friends. See *Jonson's Conversations with Drummond,* p. 20.

[3] For an interesting account of Elizabethan suits for libel, with special reference to the trial of Nicholas Udal and others concerned in the Martin Marprelate controversy, see Sir James Stephen's *History of the Criminal Law of England,* Ch. XXIV. For an account of the laws of libel in Elizabeth's reign, see Kent's *Commentaries,* II. 18. For these references the writer is indebted to William Henry Loyd, Esq., of the Philadelphia bar. The Register of the Privy Council contains accounts of difficulties which arose as the result of having represented on the stage "the persons of some gent. of good desert and quallity that are yet alive under obscure manner, but yet in such sorte as all the hearers may take notice both of the matter and the persons that are meant thereby." See *Early London*

any legal action instituted by the playwrights against Jonson, or by Jonson against the playwrights. There was undoubtedly much bitterness of feeling on both sides, but, much as the men hated each other, they sought no legal redress, for the almost libellous plays were a source of profit, and legal proceedings might have "killed the goose that laid the golden eggs."

The scene of *Poetaster* is laid in Rome, in the days of Augustus, and Jonson appears as Horace. The "Poetaster," at whom the satire is aimed, is Crispinus, who has associated with him Demetrius, "a dresser of plays," who is "to abuse Horace, and bring him in in a play" (III. 1). The great classical learning of Jonson is shown on every page, and his general attitude in the play is that of Horace (*Sat.* I. 10) in which he replies to the criticisms made on his works by his enemies, Demetrius and Tigellius. In I. 1 Ovid recites a poem which is a translation of Ovid, *Amor.*, Lib. I., *El.* 15. The song (II. 1), "If I freely may discover," is based on Martial, I. 58. In the last act is a translation of *Æneid*, IV. 160–188. There are numerous passages in which Jonson has followed very closely lines of Horace, Juvenal, and other classical writers. The climax of the satire is reached in the scene (V. 1) in which Horace gives the emetic pill to Crispinus, who with Demetrius has been condemned for attacks on Horace. This scene is an adaptation of the *Lexiphanes* of Lucian, from whom Jonson borrowed not only the idea, but also numerous phrases. *Poetaster* contains so much borrowed from classical writers that it is often difficult to say whether incidents related refer to the men of Jonson's time, or are introduced to bring the play

---

Theatres, T. Fairman Ordish, p. 90; also *Outlines of the Life of Shakespeare*, Halliwell-Phillipps, 6th ed., I. 342. How the people of the time regarded legal actions may be seen from the following passage in *The Case is Altered*, V. 4: —

Ferneze. What, are my hinds turn'd gentlemen?

Onion. Hinds, Sir! 'sblood an that word will bear an action, it shall cost us a thousand pound apiece, but we'll be revenged.

into agreement with the facts concerning Horace and his contemporaries.

Little has been added to our knowledge of the meaning of *Poetaster* since Gifford published his notes, which, although containing some mistakes, yet point out clearly the most important allusions and the true relationship of the chief characters. We are able to identify the originals of Horace (Jonson), Crispinus (Marston), and Demetrius (Dekker), but numerous less important characters remain unidentified, although in several instances there are possibly hints as to the identity of the men represented. In most cases the evidence is too slight to be of much value. It is possible that Jonson did not intend to represent his contemporaries in the characters of many of the Roman poets who appear in *Poetaster*. Although the evidence is so abundant and conclusive as to the identity of Crispinus with Marston,[1] yet critics, until the time of Gifford, who corrected the error,[2] thought it beyond question that Dekker was the man represented.[3]

Horace is avowedly Jonson, and Gifford has made clear nearly all the allusions to him in the play, the object of which was to show that what Jonson's enemies regarded to be in him arrogance, conceit, bitterness, and deserved poverty, were in reality proper self-esteem, righteous indignation, and neglected virtue.

---

[1] Jonson told Drummond that he wrote *Poetaster* on Marston (*Conversations*, p. 20), a statement that was omitted in the version of *Conversations* published in 1711 in Drummond's works. Jonson's statement was never published until 1842, and critics before that date were ignorant of it. In spite of this fact it is difficult to see how they made the mistake of supposing Crispinus to be Dekker.

[2] See note on *Poetaster*, III. 1, *Ben Jonson*, ed. Gifford, II. 453.

[3] Jonson satirized "Dekker in his *Poetaster*, 1601, under the character of Crispinus." *Shakspeare and his Times*, Drake, I. 487. "This play [*Satiromastix*] was writ on the occasion of Ben Johnson's *Poetaster*, where, under the title of Crispinus, Ben lashed our author [Dekker]." *An Account of the English Dramatick Poets*, Langbaine (ed. 1691), p. 123.

The first act of *Poetaster* is concerned almost wholly with Ovid, whose pursuit of poetry and neglect of law, in defiance of his father's wishes, gave Jonson an opportunity to ridicule the law and lawyers of his own time. He denied later[1] having attacked individuals. It may be noted in this connection, that Edward Knowell, in *Every Man in his Humour*, neglected other pursuits and gave his time to poetry, contrary to the wishes of his father; and also that Fungoso, in *Every Man out of his Humour*, neglected his study of law. We have seen that none of these characters is Marston, but it is possible that Jonson may have had Marston in mind, as we know that Marston disappointed his father's hopes in regard to becoming a lawyer.[2]

We do not know who was represented as Ovid, but Mr. Fleay suggests "Donne, who divided his attention between law and poetry, and married Anne Moore (Julia) without her father's consent."[3] Dr. Cartwright insists that Ovid is Shakespeare.[4] Tibullus and his Delia (I. 1) are thought by Mr. Fleay to be Daniel and Elizabeth Carey,[5] but this is hardly possible, since Tibullus is one of the "gallants" of Horace (III. 1), and is his friend (V. 1). Daniel, as we know, was a man against whom Jonson was bitterly hostile. The allusion to Delia is a genuine classical allusion, as the works of Tibullus are full of lines addressed to "Delia," a name given to Plautia. Mr. Fleay has expressed his opinion that Hermogenes Tigellius, "the

---

[1] In the Apologetical Dialogue, first published in 1616, but doubtless written soon after the performance of the play in 1601.

[2] In the will of Marston's father, printed by Dr. Grosart (Introduction to *Marston's Poems*), is the following passage: "to sd. son John my furniture &c. in my chambers in the Middle Temple my law books &c. to my sd. son whom I hoped would have profited by them in the study of the law but man proposeth and God disposeth, &c." This will was proved Nov. 29, 1599.

[3] *Chronicle of the English Drama*, I. 367.

[4] *Shakespeare and Jonson, Dramatic versus Wit Combats*, p. 6; see also *The North British Review*, July, 1870, p. 410, "That Shakespeare was meant by Ovid there can be little doubt." [5] *Chronicle of the English Drama*, I. 367.

excellent musician" (II. 1) and an enemy of Horace, is probably Daniel, and for this there is some evidence.[1]

Virgil, to whom is assigned a noble character, has been thought to be either Shakespeare[2] or Chapman.[3] The evidence seems to favor the latter identification, although we cannot be sure that it is correct. Gallus, a friend of Horace (III. 1), is a warrior and also a poet (V. 1). He may be the Gallus upon whom Davies wrote his Epigram.[4]

---

[1] After proving that Hedon is Daniel, Mr. Fleay says: "It seems probable ... that Hedon and Anaides ... are the same personages ... as Hermogenes Tigellius and Crispinus in *The Poetaster*," *Chronicle of the English Drama*, I. 97; but on p. 368, "Hermogenes is a musician, but not a poet (is he meant for John Daniel?)." There was a John Daniel, music-master, but whether this was the father or the brother of Samuel Daniel is an undecided question. (See *Daniel*, ed. Grosart, Memorial Introduction, I. xii.) Horace aimed *Sat.* I. 10 at Demetrius and Hermogenes Tigellius, and if Jonson gave the latter name to his enemy, Daniel, he was following his classical model.

[2] Gifford inclined to the opinion that Virgil was meant for Shakespeare. *Ben Jonson*, ed. Gifford, II. 502.

[3] Dr. Cartwright identified Virgil with Chapman (*Shakespeare and Jonson, Dramatic versus Wit Combats*, p. 6), a view shared by Professor Ward (*A History of English Dramatic Literature*, I. 565), by Mr. Fleay (*Chronicle of the English Drama*, I. 367), and by Professor Herford (*Ben Jonson*, Mermaid edition, Introduction, I. xxxiii).

> XXIV. *In Gallum.*
>
> Gallas hath beene this summer-time in Friesland
> And now return'd he speaks such warlike words,
> As, if I could their English understand,
> I feare me they would cut my throat like swords:
> He talkes of counter-scarfes and casomates,
> Of parapets, of curteneys, and palizadoes;
> Of flankers, ravelings, gabions he prates,
> And of false-brayes, and sallies and scaladoes.
> But, to requite such gulling tearmes as these,
> With words of my profession I reply;
> I tell of fourching, vouchers, and counterpleas,
> Of withermans essoynes, and champarty.
> So neither of us understanding one another,
> We part as wise as when we came together.
>   *Sir John Davies*, ed. Grosart, II. 23.

Mr. Fleay suggests to the writer that perhaps this epigram referred to Ben Jonson, who, in *Poetaster*, shifted the application to some one else.

Tucca is another version of Bobadil and Shift. Albius and Chloe are friends of Crispinus, who, at their house, sings his song (II. 1) as does also Hermogenes. Crispinus sings another song (IV. 1) and Albius sings (IV. 3) with Hermogenes and Crispinus. Albius and Chloe, as has been remarked,[1] are probably the same persons as Deliro and Fallace (*Every Man out of his Humour*), and the citizen and his wife (*Cynthia's Revels*). Mr. Fleay thinks, "Deliro possibly Monday."[2] If this were true, then Albius also would be Monday, but we have seen that Deliro is not Monday, who appears in *Every Man out of his Humour* as Puntarvolo.

The first half of Act III. consists of a dramatization of Horace (*Sat.* I. 9), and it is here that Horace first appears in the play. He is bored by the persistent attentions of Crispinus, from whom even the meeting with Fuscus Aristius[3] fails to bring relief. When Crispinus is arrested by the lictors at the instigation of Minos, Horace is enabled to escape from his tormentor, and the remainder of the act is concerned with Crispinus, Tucca, the Pyrgi, and Histrio; at the close of the act Demetrius appears. Crispinus was identified for the lictors by his "ash-coloured feather." Rufus Laberius Crispinus[4]

---

[1] Above, p. 65.
[2] *Chronicle of the English Drama*, I. 360.
[3] Fuscus (swarthy) Aristius is mentioned as a dear friend by Horace in his Satire, so there is probably no allusion in this character to any contemporary of Jonson's. It may be worth mentioning, however, that Drayton, a friend of Jonson's, speaks of himself, in his *Legend of Robert, Duke of Normandy*, as having a "swart and melancholy face."
[4] Laberius Decimus, a writer of mimes, mentioned by Horace (*Sat.* I. 10, 6), is criticised by Aulus Gellius (XVI. cap. 7), the subject of the chapter being *Quod Laberius verba pleraque licentius petulantiusque finxit: quod multis item verbis utitur, de quibus an sit Latina quaeri solet.* Gellius, Delph. et Var., II. 892. The name Laberius was peculiarly appropriate to Marston. Crispinus was ridiculed by Horace (*Serm.* I. 1, 120): *Ne me Crispini scrinia lippi compilasse putes, verbum non amplius addam.* To these two names, in themselves sufficiently contemptuous, Jonson added Rufus.

seems to be a name invented by Jonson to show his contempt for Marston. The hair of Crispinus is ridiculed several times in the play, as, for example (II. 1), when Crispinus expresses a desire to be a poet: —

Chloe. And shall your looks change, and your hair change, and all, like these?
Crispinus. Why, a man may be a poet, and yet not change his hair, lady.
Chloe. Well, we shall see your cunning : yet, if you can change your hair, I pray do.

Another personal allusion to Marston is the constant ridicule of the fact that he was of gentle birth.

Chloe. Are you a gentleman born?
Crispinus. That I am, lady ; you shall see mine arms if it please you.
Chloe. No, your legs do sufficiently shew you are a gentleman born, sir ; for a man borne upon little legs is always a gentleman born.[1]

In the following passages also Crispinus boasts of his gentility.

Crispinus. Gramercy, good Horace. Nay, we are new turned poet, too, which is more ; and a satirist, too, which is more than that : I write just in thy vein, I. I am for your odes, or your sermons, or anything indeed ; we are a gentleman besides ; our name is Rufus Laberius Crispinus ; we are a pretty Stoic, too.
Horace. To the proportion of your beard, I think it, sir.[2]
Tucca (to Histrio). Go, and be acquainted with him [Crispinus] then ; he is a gentleman parcel-poet, you slave ; his father was a man of worship, I tell thee.[3]

Gifford has observed that Dekker, in *The Guls Horne-Booke*, probably refers, in the following passage, to these various personal allusions to Marston : —

Now Sir, if the writer be a fellow that hath either epigrammd you,[4] or hath had a flirt at your mistris,[5] or hath brought either your feather, or

---

[1] II. 1. Little legs were a sign of gentle birth; see above, p. 72.
[2] III. 1.   [3] III. 1.
[4] Jonson's Epigrams 49, 68, and 100, all on Playwright, probably refer to Marston.
[5] The mistress of Anaides (*Cynthia's Revels*) is Moria (folly).

your red-beard, or your little legs, &c., on the stage, you shall disgrace him worse than by tossing him in a blancket,[1] or giving him the bastinado in a Taverne, if, in the middle of his play (bee it Pastoral or Comedy, Morall or Tragedie) you rise with a screwd and discontented face from your stool to be gone.[2]

Marston's gentility is an object of ridicule in the passage (II. 1) in which Crispinus describes his coat of arms.[3]

> My name is Crispinus or Cri-spinas[4] indeed; which is well expressed in my arms: a face crying *in chief;* and beneath it a bloody toe between three thorns *pungent.*

Mr. Fleay says of this: "Marston, as well as Crispinus, is here indicated. *Mars* is red, or bloody (compare *Mars ochre*), and *toen* is toes: together forming Marston. Both puns are equally bad."[5] Dr. Brinsley Nicholson thought this "a grotesque description of the true arms of Marston — a fesse ermine between three fleurs de lis argent. As, however, it would have been too perilous in those days of old gentility to ridicule too closely or markedly an honored heraldic device, Jonson, with viciously spiteful malice, added in chief 'a face crying,' and in so doing managed to mark out his opponent more distinctively. It may have been suggested to him by the long melancholy face of the greyhound, which is, I believe, the Marston crest; but it was an addition which became, as it were, a new and personal grant to the holder in recognition of his glorious achievement, in that he, the upholder of the honor of an old coat, had

---

[1] Horace (Jonson) is in *Satiromastix* tossed in a blanket, as a punishment for his attacks on Crispinus and others.

[2] *Dekker*, ed. Grosart, II. 253.

[3] Compare the description of Sogliardo's arms, *Every Man out of his Humour*, III. 1. See above, p. 61.

[4] Dekker parodies this in *Satiromastix* with Crispin-asse. *Dekker*, reprint Pearson, I. 212.

[5] *Shakespeare Manual*, p. 312.

taken, like Dekker, a public beating."[1] Dr. Grosart expresses a divergent opinion and says : " The 'arms' assigned to Crispinus is a mere 'canting coat,' and not very creditable fooling, with reference to the farcical name, and not corresponding with Marston's arms. These are properly blazoned thus : Sable, a fesse dancettée ermine between three fleurs de lis argent. Crest, a demi greyhound sable gorged, with a collar dancettée ermine."[2] Dr. Grosart doubts Dr. Nicholson's explanation, "that the fesse dancettée and three fleurs de lis in Marston's arms gave rise to Jonson's conceit and parody, 'a bloody toe between three thorns.'"[3]

Attention has been called several times[4] to common mistakes concerning Dekker's connection with the quarrel of Jonson and Marston. The only representation of Dekker in Jonson's plays is the character Demetrius in *Poetaster*. He appears for the first time at the close of Act III., and when he enters is unknown to all but Histrio, who informs Tucca that the stranger is "one Demetrius, a dresser of plays about the town here ; we have hired him to abuse Horace, and bring him in in a play." Tucca had only a short time before made the acquaintance of Histrio, who was hailed as he was passing. Histrio belongs to some company for which Demetrius was to write a play. Crispinus is recommended to Histrio's company by Tucca. Histrio gives as a reason for attacking Horace, " It will get us a huge deal of money." An examination of *Poetaster* shows that it is not at all impossible that Jonson did not originally intend to mention Dekker, with whom he had no quarrel, but that after *Poetaster* was well advanced in prepara-

---

[1] *Notes and Queries*, Series 4, VII. 469. The public beating is referred to by Jonson, who told Drummond that "he beat Marston." *Jonson's Conversations with Drummond*, pp. 11, 20.

[2] *Marston's Poems*, ed. Grosart, Introduction.

[3] *ibid.*

[4] Above, pp. 46, 51.

tion, although it was written in fifteen weeks, Jonson learned of the plan to "untruss" him, and in order to forestall the attack added the lines of Demetrius. The omission of a few lines (III. 1), and the alteration of a few others (V. 1) would eliminate Demetrius from the play without in any way affecting the play as an arraignment of Marston, the "poetaster," against whom Jonson had been bitterly hostile for three years. Tucca suggests to Histrio (III. 1) that Crispinus shall help Demetrius in the preparation of his play attacking Horace, but Histrio replies that Demetrius can do it "impudently enough." . . . "He has one of the most overflowing rank wits in Rome." Crispinus declares (IV. 4), "I'll write nothing in it but innocence, because I may swear I am innocent." Jonson thus exonerates Marston from any share in the actual writing of *Satiromastix*. Dekker was the "journeyman" (IV. 4) "hired to abuse Horace" (III. 1), but Crispinus, Tucca, and other enemies of Jonson were responsible for the plan. Dekker was a rapid writer,[1] well known as a "dresser of plays,"[2] and this was probably the reason he was selected to write a reply to *Poetaster*.

The fact that the company to which Histrio belonged had hired Demetrius to abuse Horace in a play, naturally connects itself with the fact that Dekker's *Satiromastix* was performed by the Chamberlain's company at the Globe Theatre.[3] Tucca's remarks to Histrio (III. 1) are significant :—

---

[1] *The Seven Deadly Sins of London*, 1606, 4to, has on the title-page Dekker's boast, *Opus septem Dierum*.

[2] Dekker's name appears frequently in *Henslowe's Diary* in connection with the remodelling of old plays.

[3] The title-page of the quarto (1602) states that *Satiromastix* was "presented publikely, by the Right Honorable, the Lord Chamberlaine his Servants; and privately, by the Children of Paules." The latter company produced Marston's plays, *Jack Drum*, *Antonio and Mellida*, and *Antonio's Revenge*. Histrio was not one of the "Children of Paules," for, if he had been, Tucca would not have needed to introduce Crispinus, or offer his services.

I hear you'll bring me o' the stage there : you'll play me, they say ; I shall be presented by a sort of copper-laced scoundrels of you : life of Pluto! an you stage me, stinkard, your mansions shall sweat for 't, your tabernacles, varlets, your Globes, and your Triumphs.

Tucca was brought on the stage at the Globe in *Satiromastix*. When Tucca told Histrio (III. 1) : "they say you have nothing but Humours, Revels, and Satires," referring to Jonson's plays, Histrio replied : "No, I assure you, captain, not we. They are on the other side of Tyber." Although Jonson's *Every Man in his Humour* and *Every Man out of his Humour* were produced by the Chamberlain's company, the former at the Curtain, the latter at the Globe, yet Jonson's next play, *Cynthia's Revels*, was produced at Blackfriars, his connection with the Chamberlain's company having ceased. Histrio, if a member of the Chamberlain's company, was correct in saying that the "Humours, Revels, and Satires" were now "on the other side of Tyber." Tucca and the two Pyrgi belonged to another company for which Crispinus was a writer. This company may have been the Children of Paul's, for whom Marston had been writing. Histrio and Æsop (who is punished V. 1) belong to some company hostile to Horace. That this was probably the same company as Sir Oliver Owlet's men in *Histriomastix*[1] is indicated by Jonson's applying to Histrio's company the lines sung by the players in *Histriomastix* : —

> Besides we that travel, with pumps full of gravel,
> Made all of such running leather,
> That once in a week, new masters we seeke,
> And never can hold together.[2]

Tucca says to Histrio (III. 1) : —

If he [Crispinus] pen for thee once, thou shalt not need to travel with thy pumps full of gravel any more, after a blind jade and a hamper, and stalk upon boards and barrel heads to an old cracked trumpet.

---

[1] See above, pp. 34, 42.   [2] *Histriomastix*, II. ll. 251-254.

Histrio's company "have Fortune and the good year" on their side, a remark applicable to the connection between the Admiral's company and the Fortune Theatre, but Tucca mentions the Globe, at which he was actually "presented." Critics are divided in their opinions as to the identity of Histrio's company, and the same two views are held as in the case of Sir Oliver Owlet's men. Mr. Fleay maintains[1] that Histrio was a member of Pembroke's company, while Professor Wood,[2] adopting the view of Simpson,[3] argues to prove that Histrio belonged to the Chamberlain's men.

The story of Ovid and Julia is made prominent in Act IV., and the balcony scene between Ovid and Julia reminds the reader of the similar scene in *Romeo and Juliet*.[4]

The last act of *Poetaster* contains Jonson's final attack on Marston. Crispinus, the "brisk Poetaster," and Demetrius, "his poor journeyman," are arraigned before Cæsar for their attacks on Horace. The indictment is read and the accused plead "not guilty." Papers are produced which Crispinus and Demetrius acknowledge having written. The lines which Crispinus admits are his, are taken from *Antonio and Mellida, Antonio's Revenge, Satires, The Scourge of Villanie,* and *Jack Drum*.[5] Demetrius admits having written some lines which are, as Gifford remarks, "assuredly meant to ridicule the loose and

---

[1] *Chronicle of the English Drama*, I. 368; see also *ibid.*, II. 70, 71, and *History of the Stage*, Fleay, pp. 137, 138, 158.

[2] See above, p. 34, note 3.

[3] See *The School of Shakspere*, II. 11, 89.

[4] It is difficult to understand the reasoning by which Dr. Cartwright reached the following conclusion: "That there may be no mistake, that Ovid is and shall be Shakespeare, the whole of the last scene in the fourth act is a parody on the third and fifth scenes in the third act of *Romeo and Juliet*." *Shakespeare and Jonson, Dramatic versus Wit Combats*, p. 6.

[5] Gifford identified the passages from Marston's works, except those from *Jack Drum*, which are given by Simpson. *School of Shakspere*, II. 128. Gifford has noted also the ridicule of Marston's style in the lines spoken by the two Pyrgi in Act III. (See *Ben Jonson*, ed. Gifford, II. 457, 517-530.)

desultory style of Dekker; though here, too, something of Marston is suffered to appear." *Satiromastix, or the Untrussing of the Humorous Poet* is referred to in the lines of Demetrius :—

> Our Muse is in mind for th' untrussing a poet,
> I slip by his name for most men do know it :
> A critic that all the world bescumbers
> With Satirical humours and lyrical numbers.
> And for the most part himself doth advance
> With much self-love, and more arrogance.
> And, but that I would not be thought a prater,
> I could tell you he were a translator.
> I know the authors from whence he has stole,
> And could trace him too[1] but that I understand
>   them not full and whole.
> The best note I can give you to know him by,
> Is, that he keeps gallants' company :
> Whom I could wish, in time should him fear,
> Lest after they buy repentance too dear.

In this passage Jonson anticipates the charges made against him in *Satiromastix*. Crispinus and Demetrius are found guilty of having slandered Horace. Before sentence is pronounced, Horace is permitted by Cæsar to give to Crispinus an emetic pill.

Marston's vocabulary had been an object of ridicule to Jonson ever since Marston's attack on the "new-minted epithets,"[2] but no former ridicule was so severe as that contained in the scene in which the emetic pill produces the desired effect on Crispinus, who, like Lexiphanes, disgorges the words that characterized his literary style. Many of the words here ridiculed by Jonson have been identified in Marston's works.[3]

---

[1] See above, p. 79. This is the same charge that was made by Anaides in *Cynthia's Revels*, III. 2.   [2] See above, p. 4.

[3] Crispinus disgorged in all thirty words, some of which were used in phrases. Twenty of the words are to be found in *The Scourge of Villanie, Jack Drum, Antonio and Mellida*, and *Antonio's Revenge*. For a list of passages in which these words are used, see *Chronicle of the English Drama*, Fleay, II. 73. The following words have not been found in Marston's works: retrograde, spurious, inflate, turgidous, ventosity, oblatrant, furibund, fatuate, prorumped, obstupefact. " Retro-

Sentence is pronounced on Crispinus and Demetrius, but for the latter Horace has asked mercy. "The oath for good behaviour" is administered to both, and they are made to swear that they will never again "malign, traduce, or detract the person or writings of Quintus Horatius Flaccus, or any other eminent man." They are forbidden ambitiously to affect "the title of the Untrussers or Whippers of the Age." The men put under oath not to attack Horace are the two men, Marston and Dekker, who attacked Jonson in plays.

Poetaster is Jonson's acknowledged reply to the numerous attacks that had been made upon him during a period of three years.[1] In this play Jonson anticipated and replied to the charges brought against him in Dekker's *Satiromastix*, a play at that time not yet acted. So far as Jonson was concerned "The War of the Theatres" was ended, although peace was not declared. *Satiromastix* was a direct reply to all of Jonson's early satirical comedies, while in Marston's *What You Will*, we can still hear, as it were, the rumbling of the storm which had just passed over. Marston and Jonson both contributed to Chester's *Love's Martyr*, 1601. In 1604 Jonson and Marston collaborated with Chapman in the writing of *Eastward Ho*, a play for which they all went to jail,[2] and in the same year we find Marston dedicating his *Malcontent*, "Benjamino Jonsonio, poetae elegantissimo, gravissimo, amico suo, candido et cordato."

---

grade" is ridiculed several times by Jonson. It is one of the words of Amorphus, who says to Morphides, "You must be *retrograde*." *Cynthia's Revels*, V. 2. Drayton, in his Elegy *Of his Lady's not coming to London*, says, "or you delight else to be *retrograde*." The word was evidently in not uncommon use, for we find *A Booke of the Seven Planets, or seven wandring motives of William Alablaster's Wit Retrograded or removed by John Racster 1598*. "Reciprocal," a word ridiculed by Jonson in *Every Man out of his Humour*, IV. 4, and *Cynthia's Revels*, I. 1, and IV. 1, is used by Marston in *The Malcontent* (1604), II. 2. "Ventosity" is one of Clove's "fustian" expressions in *Every Man out of his Humour*, III. 1. See above, p. 51.

[1] See Apologetical Dialogue.   [2] See above, p. 105, note 2.

IX.

SATIROMASTIX.

SATIROMASTIX, written by Dekker at the instigation of Marston and others, who had been satirized by Jonson, was a reply to *Poetaster*.[1] It seems probable that Dekker was at work on a play dealing with the story of Sir Walter Terill, when Marston suggested the immediate reply to Jonson's play. Horace, Crispinus, Demetrius, Tucca, and Asinius[2] are borrowed from *Poetaster*, and are quite out of place in Dekker's play, the scene of which is at the court of William Rufus. It is perfectly evident that the "Untrussing of the Humorous Poet" was no part of Dekker's original design.

When Jonson referred to Dekker as a "play-dresser" and "journeyman"[3] poet, he used terms which were particularly applicable to the author of *Satiromastix*. Attempts to identify William Rufus,[4] Sir Rees ap Vaughan, and other characters

---

[1] The Chamberlain's company, which produced *Satiromastix* in 1601, after *Poetaster*, had presented *Every Man out of his Humour*, the first play of Jonson's in which Marston was attacked. Jonson's next two plays were produced by the Chapel children at Blackfriars.

[2] Asinius Bubo in *Satiromastix* is not the same character as Asinius Lupus in *Poetaster*. The name, however, was borrowed by Dekker.

[3] *Poetaster*, V. 1; IV. 4.

[4] Reference has been made several times to absurd identifications of characters in the various plays discussed. Shakespeare has been identified by critics in at least one character in almost every play. The writer in *The North British Review* (July, 1870, p. 416) thinks Shakespeare is represented as William Rufus in *Satiro-*

than those borrowed from *Poetaster*, leave out of consideration the fact that there is no real connection between the two sets of characters. In the present discussion we are concerned only with those portions of the play in which Jonson is ridiculed as Horace. Attention has been called to the mistakes concerning Dekker's connection with "The War of the Theatres." [1] It is noticeable that Demetrius (Dekker) takes no part in the abuse of Horace, a task left almost wholly to Tucca. Many of the lines of Demetrius express admiration for the really good qualities of Horace — an admiration which was probably genuine on the part of Dekker. The three comedies in which Jonson attacked Marston are each referred to several times.

Jonson's Epigrams are mentioned frequently,[2] and his Epithalamiums, of which we have three examples, are also spoken of in several passages.[3]

Jonson's experience as a bricklayer was not forgotten by his enemies, and in *Satiromastix* he is twitted with it: —

---

mastix. Dr. Cartwright says: "William Rufus, 'learning's true Mæcenas, poesy's king,' it may be presumed, was the ignorant William Shakespeare. . . . The wits of Elizabeth were not asleep. In this comedy Shakespeare is King William and Lyly is Sir Vaughan ap Rees: the remark of Tucca, 'be not so tart my precious Metheglin,' identifies Lyly with Amorphus, reminding us of the Metheglin and 'Pythagoricall breeches' in *Cynthia's Revels*." *Shakespeare and Jonson, Dramatic versus Wit Combats*, p. 52. In *Manningham's Diary*, p. 39, Camden Society publications, is an anecdote showing that William the Conqueror was, on at least one occasion, a nickname of Shakespeare.

[1] See above, pp. 46, 51, 67, 68, 70, 107, 113.

[2] *Dekker*, I.; *Satiromastix*, pp. 195, 212, 221, 241. (All references to *Satiromastix* are to the pages in the edition published by Pearson in 1873. The play is not divided into acts and scenes.) Cf. Jonson's Epigrams on *Playwright* (Marston), 49, 68, 100; *True Soldiers*, 108 (also in Apologetical Dialogue appended to *Poetaster*); *Shift*, 12; *Poet-Ape*, 56.

[3] *Satiromastix*, pp. 190, 192, 215, 241. The three Epithalamiums of Jonson's that we have are *Underwoods 93 Epithalamium*, celebrating the nuptials of Mr. Hierome Weston and Lady Frances Stewart, and the two contained in *The Masque of Hymen* and *The Hue and Cry after Cupid*.

Asinius (to Horace). Nay, I ha more news, ther's Crispinus and his Jorneyman Poet Demetrius Fannius[1] too, they sweare they'll bring your life and death upon'th stage like a Bricklayer in a play.[2]

Tucca calls Horace a "poor lyme and hayre rascall,"[3] and a "foule-fisted Morter-treader."[4]

Sir Vaughan (to Horace). Two urds Horace about your eares: how chance it passes, that you bid God boygh to an honest trade of building Symneys, and laying downe Brickes, for a worse handicraftnes, to make nothing but railes;[5]

When it is suggested that Horace be tossed in a blanket, Tucca asks him: —

... dost stampe mad Tamberlaine, dost stampe? thou thinkst th'ast Morter under thy feete, dost?[6]

A pun is intended in the following: —

Sir Vaughan. Horace and Bubo, pray send an answere into his Majesties eares why you go thus in Ovid's *Morter-Morphesis* and strange fashions of apparell.[7]

The fact that Jonson was saved from hanging by being able to "con his neck-verse," after he had been sentenced for killing in a duel Gabriel Spencer, a player,[8] is thus alluded to by Dekker: —

---

[1] Dekker refers several times to titles given by Jonson to Crispinus and Demetrius. Horace says: "As for Crispinus, that Crispin-asse, and Fannius, his play-dresser" (*Satiromastix*, p. 212). Jonson interpreted Crispinus as "Cri-spinas" (see above, p. 112), and this is Dekker's retort. Demetrius (Dekker) is called "a dresser of plays" (*Poetaster*, III. 1) and "play-dresser" (*Poetaster*, V. 1).

[2] *Satiromastix*, p. 195. For the allusion to bringing Jonson on the stage, see *Poetaster*, III. 1, and IV. 4.

[3] *ibid.*, p. 199. Emulo, in *Patient Grissil*, II. 1, is asked: "Where's the lime and hair?" See above, p. 68. [6] *ibid.*

[4] *ibid.*, p. 234. [7] *ibid.*, p. 258.

[5] *ibid.*, p. 243. [8] See above, p. 7.

Asinius (to Horace). Answere, as God judge me Ningle, for thy wit thou mayst answer any Justice of peace in England I warrant; thou writ'st in a most goodly big hand too, I like that, I readst as leageably as some that have bin sav'd by their neck-verse.[1]

Tucca. The best verse that ever I knew him hacke out, was his white neck-verse.[2]

Tucca (to Horace). Holde, holde up thy hand, I ha seene the day thou didst not scorne to hold up thy golles.[3]

This is evidently a reference to Jonson's trial for murder. When the indictment was read the accused had to hold up his hands. We have here also a reply to the treatment of Crispinus and Demetrius in *Poetaster* (V. 1), where they are made to "hold up their spread golls." Horace is made to do what he had made others do.

Tucca (to Horace). Art not famous enough yet, my mad Horastratus, for killing a Player, but thou must eate men alive?[4]

Tucca (to Horace). Thou art the true arraign'd Poet, and shouldst have been hang'd, but for one of these part-takers, these charitable Copper-lac'd Christians that fetch thee out of Purgatory (Players I meane) Theaterians pouch-mouth, Stage-walkers:[5]

Sir Vaughan (to Horace). *Inprimis*, you shall sweare by Phoebus and the halfe a score Muses lacking one: not to sweare to hang your selfe, if you thought any Man, Ooman or Silde, could write Playes and Rimes, as well-favour'd ones as your selfe.

Tucca. Well sayd, hast brought him toth gallowes already.[6]

Crispinus (to Horace). . . . were thy warpt soule, put in a new molde
Ide weare thee as a Jewell set in golde.

Sir Vaughan. And Jewels, Master Horace, must be hang'd you know.[7]

---

[1] *Satiromastix*, p. 194. [3] *ibid.*, p. 203.
[2] *ibid.*, p. 241. [4] *ibid.*, p. 234.
[5] *ibid.*, p. 244. It is thought by some that the allusion is to Jonson's difficulties in consequence of his duel, and that it was through the intervention of Shakespeare that he was released. See Collier's *Memoirs of Actors*, p. xx, Shakespeare Society publications; also *Early London Theatres*, T. Fairman Ordish, pp. 190-3. There is no proof that Shakespeare was the man, although he may have been.
[6] *Satiromastix*, p. 261. [7] *ibid.*, p. 245.

Jonson served in the Low Countries, and this is referred to by Sir Quintilian, who asks, concerning Horace: —

> What Gentleman is this in the Mandilian, a soldyer?

To this question Sir Vaughan replies: —

> No, tho he has a very bad face for a souldier, yet he has as desperate a wit as ever any Scholler went to cuffes for;[1]

The "bad face" was Jonson's "rocky-face," as he called it in the lines on *My Picture Left in Scotland*.[2] Another reference to Jonson's having been a soldier, and also to his having killed his adversary in a duel, is the warning of Horace to Tucca, "Holde Capten, tis knowne that Horace is valliant and a man of the sword."[3] This is a quotation from *Poetaster* (IV. 4) where Pyrgus tells Tucca, "Horace is a man of the sword," and Crispinus adds, "They say he's valiant." Jonson's career as an actor is referred to by Tucca on two occasions.

> *Horace.* No Captaine, Ile weare anything.
> *Tucca.* I know thou wilt, I know th' art an honest low minded Pigmey, for I ha seene thy shoulders lapt in a Plaiers old cast Cloake, like a Slie knave as thou art: and when thou ranst mad for the death of Horatio:[4] thou borrowedst a gowne of Roscius the Stager (that honest Nicodemus) and sentest it home lowsie, didst not?[5]

---

[1] *Satiromastix*, p. 215.

[2] *Underwoods*, VII. Jonson's face is a subject of jest elsewhere. Dicace says: "That same Horace me thinkes has the most ungodly face, by my Fan; it lookes for all the world, like a rotten russet Apple, when tis bruiz'd." Miniver declares, "Its cake and pudding to me to see his face make faces, when hee reades his Songs and Sonnets." *Satiromastix*, p. 241. "Horace [*i.e.*, Roman Horace] had not his face puncht full of Oylet-holes, like the cover of a warming-pan." *Ibid.*, p. 260.

[3] *Satiromastix*, p. 234. Jonson killed "ane enemie" in the Low Countries, an incident which is included in the reference here. *Jonson's Conversations with Drummond*, p. 18. See above, p. 7.

[4] Hieronimo becomes mad after the death of Horatio in *The Spanish Tragedy* II. Jonson acted the part of Hieronimo. [5] *Satiromastix*, p. 202.

In another passage Tucca says to Horace : "Thou hast been at Parris garden hast not?" and Horace replies, " Yes Captaine, I ha plaide Zulziman there."

Tucca remarks : —

... thou hast forgot how thou amblest (in leather pilch) by a play-wagon, in the high way, and tooks't mad Jeronimoes part, to get service among the Mimickes: [1]

The fact that Jonson was at this time a Roman Catholic[2] is thus noticed by Dekker, who makes Tucca say to Horace,—

Nay, I smell what breath is to come from thee, thy answer is, that there's no faith to be helde with Heritickes and Infidels, and therfore thou swear'st anie thing: [3]

The meaning of the speeches about baldness is unknown, unless indeed there be in them an allusion to Jonson's licentiousness.[4] The identity of Asinius is also unknown.

Most of the allusions in *Satiromastix* are perfectly clear to any one familiar with Jonson's early comedies, and it is therefore not necessary in the present discussion to point out any but the most important. Some of the purely personal references to Jonson have been mentioned, and we proceed to notice next those passages in which Dekker replies to passages in Jonson's plays. The characters in which Jonson had represented himself are thus referred to : —

Tucca (to Horace). No, you starv'd rascal, thou 't bite off mine eares then, you must have three or foure suites of names, when like a lowsie Pe-

---

[1] *Satiromastix*, p. 229.

[2] Jonson was in prison in consequence of his duel (1598). "Then took he his religion by trust, of a priest who visited him in prisson. Thereafter he was 12 yeares a Papist." *Jonson's Conversations with Drummond*, p. 19.

[3] *Satiromastix*, p. 235.

[4] Mr. Fleay suggests that Gabriel Harvey "wrote against baldness: this may throw some light on the Jonson speech in Dekker's *Satiromastix*." *Chronicle of the English Drama*, II. 142.

diculous vermin th'ast but one suite to thy backe: you must be call'd Asper, and Criticus, and Horace, thy tytle's longer a reading then the Stile a the big Turkes: Asper,[1] Criticus,[2] Quintus Horatius[3] Flaccus.[4]

The titles of *Every Man in his Humour* and *Every Man out of his Humour*, as well as Jonson's theory of "humours," are glanced at in the epithet "humorous," applied to Horace by Dekker.

The general relation of Jonson's plays to the times is indicated by the following words of Tucca, in which he mentions by name two of the plays: —

A Gentleman or an honest Cittizen shall not Sit in your pennie-bench Theaters, with his Squirrel by his side cracking nuttes ; nor sneake into a Taverne with his Mermaid ; but he shall be Satyr'd and Epigram'd upon, and his humour must run upo'th Stage: you'll ha *Every Gentleman in's humour*, and *Every Gentleman out on's humour*.[5]

When the King says, "True poets are with Arte and Nature Crownd,"[6] we have perhaps a reference to the Prologue to *Every Man in his Humour*, in which Jonson declares: —

> Though need make many poets, and some such
> As art and nature have not bettered much ;
> Yet ours for want hath not so loved the stage, etc.

Crispinus says that Horace "calles himselfe the whip of men."[7] This is probably an allusion to the Induction of *Every Man out of his Humour*, in which Asper declares: —

> . . . with an armed and resolved hand,
> I'll strip the ragged follies of the time
> Naked as at their birth . . . and with a whip of steel,
> Print wounding lashes in their iron ribs.

---

[1] *Every Man out of his Humour.*
[2] *Cynthia's Revels*, quarto. In the folio the name is Crites.
[3] *Poetaster.*
[4] *Satiromastix*, p. 200.   [6] *ibid.*, p. 256.
[5] *ibid.*, p. 234.   [7] *ibid.*

Horace is threatened with having to "sit at the upper ende of the Table, a 'th left hand of Carlo Buffon,"[1] a fate which shows that *Every Man out of his Humour*, with its satire on Marston, as Carlo, was not forgotten. The Palinode, sung by the disgraced maskers at the conclusion of *Cynthia's Revels*, seems to have been greatly resented, for it is alluded to several times by Dekker. Horace speaks of "the Palinode which I meane to stitch to my Revels";[2] he is called "Palinodicall rimester,"[3] and Sir Vaughan refers to the "Polinoddyes"[4] and "Callin-oes."[5] The oath which Horace takes at the end of the play was suggested not only by the oath administered to Crispinus and Demetrius in *Poetaster*, but also by the Palinode. Asinius Bubo, "Horace's Ape," used "connive," and was ridiculed for it by his barber, who said:—

> Master Asinius Bubo, you have eene Horaces wordes as right as if he had spit them into your mouth.[6]

As Gifford pointed out, the word "connive" was used by other dramatic writers, without the preposition."[7] Jonson, however, makes Moria say, in *Cynthia's Revels* (IV. 1), "therefore there is more respect requirable howsoe'er you seem to connive."

Jonson wrote in the Prologue to *Cynthia's Revels*:—

> Our doubtful author hopes this is their sphere,
> And therefore opens he himself to those,
> To other weaker beams his labours close,
> As loth to prostitute their virgin strain,
> To every vulgar and adulterate brain.
> In this alone, his Muse her sweetness hath,
> She shuns the print of any beaten path:
> And proves new ways to come to learned eares:

---

[1] *Satiromastix*, p. 263.
[2] *ibid.*, p. 194.
[3] *ibid.*, p. 234.
[4] *ibid.*, p. 241.
[5] *ibid.*, p. 260.
[6] *ibid.*, p. 212.
[7] *Jonson*, ed. Gifford, II. 300.

Dekker makes Horace say :—

> That we to learned eares should sweetly sing,
> But to the vulger and adulterate braine
> Should loath to prostitute our Virgin straine.[1]

When Sir Vaughan says —

Horace is ambition, and does conspire to bee more hye and tall as God a mightie made him, wee'll carry his terrible person to Court, and there before his Majestie Dub, or what you call it, dip his Muse in some licour, and christen him, or dye him, into collours of a Poet.[2]

we have perhaps an allusion to the differences between Daniel, who was poet-laureate, and Jonson, who wished to be. Hedon (Daniel) is called "ambition" by Philautia in *Cynthia's Revels*, IV. 1.

When *Cynthia's Revels* was performed at court, it evidently failed to meet with approval, for when the quarto was published (1601) it bore on the title-page the motto, —

> Quod non dant proceres, dabit histrio —
> Haud tamen invideas vati, quem pulpita pascunt.

It is perhaps to the state of affairs indicated by this motto that Sir Vaughan refers, when he tells Horace —

. . . when your Playes are misse-likt at Court, you shall not crye Mew like a Pusse-cat, and say you are glad you write out of the Courtiers Element.[3]

One of the most interesting references to *Cynthia's Revels* is in the passage in which Dekker identifies Demetrius with Hedon.[4]

> *Horace.* That same Crispinus is the silliest Dor, and Fannius the
>   slightest cobweb-lawne peece of a Poet, oh God !
> Why should I care what every Dor doth buz
> In credulous eares, it is a crowne to me,
> That the best judgements can report me wrong'd.

---

[1] *Satiromastix*, p. 213.
[2] *ibid.*, p. 246.
[3] *ibid.*, p. 262.
[4] See above, p. 80.

Asinius. I am one of them that can report it.
Horace. I thinke but what they are, and am not mov'd.
The one a light voluptuous Reveler,
The other, a strange arrogating puffe
Both impudent, and arrogant enough.
Asinius. S'lid, do not Criticus Revel in these lynes, ha, Ningle, ha?
Horace. Yes, they're mine owne.[1]

The four men satirized in *Cynthia's Revels* are called by Jonson "Arachnean workers," and a "knot of spiders," and their conversation is called "cobweb stuff."[2] It is this to which Dekker alludes in the expression "cobweb-lawne peece of a Poet." Horace quotes, with slight changes, lines of Crites concerning Hedon (Daniel) and Anaides (Marston).

Crites. What should I care what every dor doth buz
In credulous ears? It is a crown to me
That the best judgments can report me wronged;
. . . .
'Tis Hedon and Anaides, alas, then
I think but what they are, and am not stirred.
The one a light voluptuous reveller,
The other, a strange arrogating puff,
Both impudent, and ignorant enough.[3]

Passages in *Poetaster* also are quoted and parodied by Dekker, and there are numerous allusions to the play. When Horace is discovered in his study, he is composing a poem in which Dekker ridicules some lines recited by Horace in *Poetaster*, III. 1.

Swell me a bowl with lusty wine,
Till I may see the plump Lyæus swim
Above the brim:
I drink as I would write,
In flowing measure filled with flame and sprite.

---

[1] *Satiromastix*, p. 195.
[2] *Cynthia's Revels*, III. 2.
[3] *ibid*.

Dekker ridicules particularly the last line and the word "swim," and makes Horace say :—

> To thee whose forehead swels with Roses
> . . . .
> For I to thee and thine immortall name,
> In flowing numbers fild with spright and flame.[1]

The book that Asinius reads "smels of Rose-leaves,"[2] which may be because Horace dips his "pen in distilde Roses."[3]

There are several allusions to the pills given to Crispinus (*Poetaster*, V. 1), as, for example, where Crispinus says to Horace :—

> . . . when your dastard wit will strike at men
> In corners, and in riddles folde the vices
> Of your best friends, you must not take to heart,
> If they take off all gilding from their pilles
> And onley offer you the bitter Coare.[4]

A little further on Crispinus says :—

> We come like your Phisitions, to purge
> Your sicke and daungerous minde of her disease.[5]

The scene in *Poetaster* in which the pills are given to Crispinus was adapted from the *Lexiphanes* of Lucian—a fact which is referred to by Tucca when he calls Horace Lucian.[6]

Jonson's shabby clothes were frequently ridiculed by his enemies. Tucca calls Horace "that Judas yonder that walkes in Rug,"[7] referring to the rug gown of the scholar. Jonson had referred to the clothes worn by Crispinus and Demetrius :

---

[1] *Satiromastix*, p. 191. The lines omitted represent Horace in difficulties over his rhymes.
[2] *ibid.*, p. 199.
[3] *ibid.*, p. 197.
[4] *ibid.*
[5] *ibid.*, p. 198.
[6] *ibid.*, p. 235.
[7] *ibid.*, p. 199.

Horace (to Crispinus). Yes, sir; your satin sleeve begins to fret at the rug that is underneath it, I do observe; and your ample velvet bases are not without evident stains of a hot disposition naturally.[1]

Histrio (of Demetrius). O, sir, his doublet's a little decayed. ....[2]

Dekker had in mind these two passages when he made Tucca say to Horace —

Thou wrongst heere a good honest rascall Crispinus, and a poore varlet Demetrius Fanninus (bretheren in thine owne trade of Poetry), thou sayst Crispinus Sattin dublet is Reavel'd out heere, and that this penurious sneaker is out of elboes. ...[3]

In another passage Tucca says to Horace : —

Good Pagans, well said, they have sowed up that broken seame-rent lye of thine, that Demetrius is out at Elbowes, and Crispinus is falne out with Sattin heere, they have;

Tucca. Ist not better be out at Elbowes, then to bee a bond-slave and to goe all in Parchment as thou dost?

Horace. Parchment, Captaine? tis Perpetuana I assure you.[4]

This is perhaps a reference to the remark of Hedon concerning Crites (Jonson), —

"By this heaven I wonder at nothing more than our gentlemen ushers, that will suffer a piece of serge or perpetuana to come into the presence ...[5]

Jonson's slowness in writing his plays was evidently a common subject of jest. He stated in the Envy Prologue to *Poetaster* that he wrote the play in fifteen weeks, a statement to which Tucca refers when he says, "Will he bee fifteene weekes about this Cockatrice's egge too?"[6]

---

[1] *Poetaster*, III. 1.
[2] *ibid.*
[3] *Satiromastix*, p. 201.
[4] *ibid.*, p. 245.
[5] *Cynthia's Revels*, III. 2.
[6] *Satiromastix*, p. 202.

Tucca calls Horace a " Nastie Tortois " and says : —

> . . . you and your Itchy Poetry breake out like Christmas, but once a yeare, and then you keepe a Revelling, and Araigning and a Scratching of mens faces, as tho you were Tyber the long-tail'd Prince of Rattes, doe you?[1]

One new play each year was written by Jonson in 1598, 1599, 1600, and 1601, and the allusion to the titles of *Cynthia's Revels* and *Poetaster or his Arraignment* is apparent.[2]

The " Ooh ! " uttered by Horace[3] is a reply to the " Ooh ! " of Crispinus in *Poetaster* (V. 1).

Horace, in *Poetaster* (III. 1), refers to the poetry of Crispinus as " lewd solecisms," but in *Satiromastix* Horace will " rather breath out Solœcismes"[4] than " wound " the " worth " of Tucca.

When Tucca says to Asinius, " arise, deere Eccho, rise,"[5] we have perhaps an allusion to *Cynthia's Revels* (I. 1), where Mercury summons Echo, —

> Arise, and speak thy sorrows, Echo rise.

Marston evidently resented being called a " gentleman parcel-poet,"[6] for Tucca says " the Parcell-Poets shall Sue thy wrangling Muse in the Court of Pernassus . . . "[7]

When Horace is about to be tossed in a blanket, he asks, —

> Why, would you make me thus the ball of scorne?

and he is answered by Tucca in a passage full of allusions to *Poetaster*.

---

[1] *Satiromastix*, p. 259.
[2] *Poetaster* is referred to by name on p. 235 of *Satiromastix*.
[3] *Satiromastix*, p. 260.
[4] *ibid.*, p. 234.
[5] *ibid.*, p. 230.
[6] *Poetaster*, IV. 3.
[7] *Satiromastix*, p. 235.

Ile tell thee why, because th'ast entred Actions of assault and battery, against a companie of honourable and worshipfull Fathers of the law : you wrangling rascall, law is one of the pillers ath land, and if thou beest bound too 't (as I hope thou shalt bee) thou 't proove a skip-Jacke, thou 't be whipt. Ile tell thee why, because thy sputtering chappes yelpe, that Arrogance and Impudence and Ignoraunce, are the essentiall parts of a Courtier.[1]

In *Cynthia's Revels* (II. 1) Mercury says of Anaides (Marston) : —

> . . . he has two essential parts of the courtier, pride and ignorance. . . . 'T is Impudence itself, Anaides ;

The attack on law and lawyers, made by Jonson in *Poetaster*, was resented, and he was brought before the Lord Chief Justice for it. He was evidently put under oath not to repeat the offence. It is to this that Dekker probably refers in the following passage : —

Tucca (to Horace). I know now th'ast a number of these *Quiddits* to binde men to 'th peace: tis thy fashion to flirt Inke in everie man's face; and then to craule into his bosome, and damne thy selfe to wip 't off agen : . . . I could make thine eares burne now, by dropping into them, all those hot oathes, to which, thy selfe gav'st voluntarie fire (when thou was the man in the Moone) that thou wouldst never squib out any new Salt-peter Jestes against honest Tucca, nor those Maligo-tasters, his *Poetasters;* I could Cinocephalus, but I will not, yet thou knowst thou hast broke those oathes in print, my excellent infernall.[2]

Further reasons for tossing Horace in a blanket are thus given by Tucca : —

Ile tell thee why, because thou cryest ptrooh at worshipfull Cittizens, and cal'st them Hat-caps, Cuckolds, and banckrupts, and modest and vertuous wives punckes and cockatrices. Ile tell thee why, because th'ast arraigned two Poets against all lawe and conscience ; and not content with that, hast turn'd them amongst a company of horrible blacke Fryers.[3]

---

[1] *Satiromastix*, p. 244.   [2] *ibid.*, p. 235.   [3] *ibid.*, p. 244.

The last statement refers of course to the arraignment of Crispinus and Demetrius in *Poetaster*, which was performed at Blackfriars by the Chapel children.[1] Albius and Chloe, a citizen and his wife, are in *Poetaster* (IV. 1; IV. 3) called the names mentioned by Tucca.

Jonson made Demetrius confess that his reason for maligning Horace was —

that he kept better company, for the most part, than I ; and that better men loved him than loved me. . . .[2]

Dekker remembered this, and Horace is made to say —

They envy me because I holde more worthy company.[3]

When Demetrius appears in *Poetaster* (III. 1) Tucca has just ordered Minos and the two Pyrgi to present "the Moor." This evidently annoyed Dekker, who in *Satiromastix* says that Fannius "cut an Innocent Moore i' th middle, to serve him in twice ; and when he had done, made Poules-worke of it,[4] as for these Twynnes, these Poet-apes : Their Mimicke trickes shall serve."[5] The title "Poet-ape" offended the men to whom Jonson applied it, for when Horace has taken the oath Crispinus says to him : —

---

[1] The fact that the play was performed at Blackfriars is alluded to in the Epilogue to *Satiromastix* spoken by Tucca, who says, "I recant the opinions which I helde [*i.e.*, in *Poetaster*] of Courtiers, Ladies, and Cittizens, when once (in an assembly of Friers) I railde upon them : "

[2] *Poetaster*, V. 1. In the oath administered to Crispinus and Demetrius, they swear that they will never again malign Horace "for keeping himself in better acquaintance, or enjoying better friends."

[3] *Satiromastix*, p. 244.

[4] The allusion to the Moor is explained by Mr. Fleay as referring to *The Life and Death of Captain Thomas Stukeley*. "Dekker had patched up the play with half of one by Peele on the Moor Mahomet, and then published it." *Chronicle of the English Drama*, I. 128.

[5] *Satiromastix*, p. 212.

> That fearefull wreath, this honour is your due,
> All Poets shall be Poet-Apes but you ;[1]

The allusions to *Poetaster* are of course more numerous than those to any other play. Dekker borrowed from that play the characters concerned in the satire on Jonson, and the trial scene before William Rufus is based on the last scene in *Poetaster*. We do not know whether Dekker had ever heard or read the Apologetical Dialogue[2] which was afterwards appended to *Poetaster* in the folio of 1616, but it is probable that Jonson, when in difficulty with the lawyers for satirizing them, had made representations similar to those in the Dialogue. He claimed to have attacked only sin, and to have spared persons, and this seems to have been particularly exasperating to the men whom he had undoubtedly represented on the stage. Dekker has made much of this declaration of innocence on the part of Jonson, and in several passages Horace is upbraided for satirizing men and then denying having done so. Demetrius (Dekker) seems to have no bitterness toward Horace, but in every speech exhibits a magnanimity that is in sharp contrast to the arrogant and self-sufficient tone of Jonson's satirical plays. Mention was made above of the passage in which Dekker speaks of four men as pointing " with their fingers in one instant at one and the same man."[3] These four were the men whom Jonson had attacked in *Every Man out of his Humour* and *Cynthia's Revels*. These men probably were responsible for the writing of *Satiromastix*, for, so far as we

---

[1] *ibid.*, p. 263. The Envy Prologue to *Poetaster* asks, "Are there no players here? no poet-apes?" Epigram 56 is *On Poet Ape*, probably Marston or Dekker.

[2] Jonson tells us that the Apologetical Dialogue was "only once spoken upon the stage," but we do not know when. The note appended to the quarto, 1602, mentions an apology which the author was "restrained . . . by authority" from publishing (see above, p. 102, note 4).

[3] p. 76.

can judge from the evidence at hand, it is unlikely that Dekker would have undertaken the task on his own account.

Horace is brought before King William Rufus, and is by him turned over to Crispinus (Marston) for punishment.

> *King.* If a cleare merrit stand upon his praise,
> Reach him a Poet's Crowne (the honour'd Bayes)
> But if he claime it, wanting right thereto,
> (As many bastard Sonnes of Poesie doe)
> Race downe his usurpation to the ground.
> True Poets are with Arte and Nature Crown'd.
> But in what molde so ere this man bee cast,
> We make him thine Crispinus, wit and judgement,
> Shine in thy numbers, and thy soule I know,
> Will not goe arm'd in passion gainst thy foe :
> Therefore be thou our selfe ; whilst our selfe sit,
> But as spectator of this Sceane of wit.[1]

Throughout the play Tucca bullies Horace and abuses him. A comparison is made between a picture of the Roman Horace and one of Horace-Jonson,[2] who is thus arraigned by Crispinus : —

> Under controule of my dreade Soveraigne,
> We are thy Judges : thou that didst Arraigne,
> Art now prepar'd for condemnation ;
> Should I but bid thy Muse stand to the Barre,
> Thyselfe against her wouldst give evidence :
> For flat rebellion gainst the Sacred lawes
> Of divine Poesie : heerein most she mist,
> Thy pride and scorne made her turne Saterist,
> And not her love to vertue (as thou Preachest)
> Or should we minister strong pilles to thee :
> What lumpes of hard and indigested stuffe,
> Of bitter Satirisme, of Arrogance,
> Of Self-love, of Detraction, of a blacke

---

[1] *Satiromastix*, p. 256.
[2] cf. the two pictures introduced in *Antonio and Mellida* (see above, p. 98).

> And stinking Insolence should we fetch up?
> But none of these, we give thee what's more fit,
> With stinging nettles Crowne his stinging wit.[1]

This is the reply to the scene in which Crispinus is given the emetic pills.[2]

The oath which is administered to Horace is a reply both to the Palinode, sung by the false courtiers in *Cynthia's Revels*, and to the oath taken by Crispinus and Demetrius in *Poetaster*. With this oath the formal answer to Jonson's play ends.

---

[1] *Satiromastix*, p. 259.
[2] *Poetaster*, V. 1.

X.

WHAT YOU WILL.

THE last play of Marston's in which there is an unmistakable attack on Jonson is *What You Will*, first published in 1607.[1] We do not know when it was written, but it was probably before the reconciliation with Jonson (to whom, in 1604, Marston dedicated *The Malcontent*[2]), and after *Poetaster* (1601), which quotes from it no "fustian" words.

That the play contained personal satire is shown by the tone of the Induction spoken by Atticus, Doricus, and Philomuse, friends of the author. They refer to the presence near the stage of Sir Signior Snuff, Monsieur Mew, and Cavaliero Blirt, "three of the most-to-be-feared auditors."[3] Philomuse, the author's particular friend, defies and tries to disarm criticism by declaring that the author's spirit —

> Is higher blooded than to quake and pant
> At the report of Scoff's artillery.
> Shall he be crest-fall 'n, if some looser brain,

---

[1] The writer in *The North British Review*, July, 1870, thinks that Marston "made a study of him [Jonson] as Malevole in *The Malcontent*" (p. 402); and also that "Jonson seems to have understood the play [*Parasitaster*] as aimed at him, and as calling him both parasite and fawn" (p. 404, note 1). There seems to be no sufficient reason for either of these statements.

[2] See above, p. 118.

[3] Mr. Fleay thinks that Sir Signior Snuff, Monsieur Mew, and Cavaliero Blirt "mean Armin, Jonson, and Middleton," and that Philomuse is "Daniel, whose *Musophilus* was written 1599." *Chronicle of the English Drama*, II. 77. These identifications must stand as mere conjectures, for there seems to be no means of proving them.

> In flux of wit uncivilly befilth
> His slight composures? Shall his bosom faint,
> If drunken Censure belch out sour breath
> From Hatred's surfeit on his labour's front?[1]

The Prologue also defies criticism in saying of the author:—

> Nor labours he the favour of the rude,
> Nor offers sops unto the Stygian dog,
> To force a silence in his viperous tongues ;
> Nor cares he to insinuate the grace
> Of loath'd detraction, nor pursues the love
> Of the nice critics of this squeamish age ;
> Nor strives he to bear up with every sail
> Of floating censure : nor once dreads or cares
> What envious hand his guiltless muse hath struck.

The "envious hand" may have been Jonson's.

There are in *What You Will* two characters who, whenever they meet, engage in mutual abuse and wrangling. Lampatho and Quadratus are almost certainly representations of Marston and Jonson respectively.[2] The passage which indicates clearly the identity of Lampatho is as follows :—

> *Lampatho.* So Phœbus warm my brain, I'll rhyme thee **dead**.
> Look for the satire : if all the sour juice
> Of a tart brain can souse thy estimate
> I'll pickle thee.
> *Quadratus.* Ha! he mount Chirall on the wings of fame![3]

---

[1] This is possibly an allusion to the scene in *Poetaster* (V. 1) in which Crispinus (Marston) is made to disgorge the "fustian" words.

[2] Professor Ward is probably mistaken in his identification of Quadratus with Hall. He says: "In a scene (II. 1) the author evidently identifies the poet Lampatho Doria with himself, and the foul-mouthed Quadratus, whom Lampatho threatens to 'rhyme dead' by a 'satire,' with his adversary, Hall." *A History of English Dramatic Literature*, II. 64.

[3] cf. Induction to *Mucedorus*, "And raise his chival with a lasting fame." "Chirall" may have been printed for "chival." See Mr. Bullen's note. *Marston*, ed. Bullen, I. 349.

	A horse ! a horse ! My kingdom for a horse !![1]
	Look thee, I speak play-scraps. Bidet, I 'll down,
	Sing, sing, or stay, we 'll quaff, or anything.
	Rivo, Saint Mark, let 's talk as loose as air :
	Unwind youth's colours, display ourselves,
	So that yon envy-starved cur may yelp
	And spend his chaps at our fantasticness.
Simplicius.	O Lord, Quadratus !
Quadratus.	Away, idolater ! Why, you Don Kinsayder !
	Thou canker-eaten rusty cur ! thou snaffle
	To freer spirits !
	Thinkst thou, a libertine, an ungyved breast,
	Scorns not the shackles of thy envious clogs ?
	You will traduce us into public scorn ?
Lampatho.	By this hand I will.
Quadratus.	A foutra for thy hand, thy heart, thy brain !
	Thy hate, thy malice, envy, grinning spite !
	Shall a free-born, that holds antipathy —
Lampatho.	Antipathy !
Quadratus.	Ay, antipathy, a native hate
	Unto the curse of man, bare-pated servitude,
	Quake at the frowns of a ragg'd satirist — [2]

The fact that Lampatho is called " Don Kinsayder . . . a ragg'd satirist," is sufficient to identify him as Marston,[3] who, at the end of his note " To those that Seeme Judiciall Peru-

---

[1] *Richard III.*, V. 4. This line was parodied by Marston in the *The Scourge of Villanie*, Satire VII., " A man ! a man ! a kingdom for a man ! " and in *Parasitaster*, V. 1, " A fool, a fool, a fool, my coxcomb for a fool ! "

[2] II. 1.

[3] Mr. Bullen, while recognizing that Marston and Jonson both appear in *What You Will*, makes the strange mistake of identifying Quadratus with Marston and Lampatho with Jonson. " Quadratus' scathing ridicule of Lampatho Doria, in the first scene of the second act, was certainly aimed at some adversary of Marston's ; and there can be little doubt that this adversary was Ben Jonson " (*Marston*, ed. Bullen, I. xlvi). " Curious that Marston should apply his own *nom de plume*, ' Kinsayder,' to the adversary whom he is bullying ! " *Ibid.*, p. xlvii. It would indeed have been strange if he had. " But it is not to be doubted that Quadratus' abuse of Lampatho was levelled at Ben Jonson." *Ibid.*, p. xlviii. Mr. Bullen notices the similarity between the speeches mentioned above.

sers,"[1] prefixed to *The Scourge of Villanie*, signed himself W. Kinsayder, and who is referred to as "Monsieur Kinsayder" by the author of *The Return from Parnassus*.[2] The passage quoted above shows the relations existing between Quadratus and Lampatho throughout the play.

That Quadratus is Jonson is indicated by the following speech (II. 1) which imitates a speech of Crites in *Cynthia's Revels*, III. 2.[3]

> *Quadratus.* No, Sir ; should discreet Mastigophoros,
> Or the dear spirit acute Canaidus
> (That Aretine, that most of me beloved,
> Who in the rich esteem I prize his soul,
> I term myself) ; should these once menace me,
> Or curb my humours with well-govern'd check,
> I should with most industrious regard,
> Observe, abstain, and curb my skipping lightness.

A noteworthy encounter between Quadratus and Lampatho, in IV. 1, contains two allusions which, taken together, are almost sufficient to fix the identity of the two men.

> *Quadratus* (of Lampatho). A tassel that hangs at my purse-strings. He dogs me, and I give him scraps, and pay for his ordinary, feed him ; he liquors himself in the juice of my bounty ; and when he hath suck'd up strength of spirit he squeezeth it in my own face ; when I have refined and sharp'd his wits with good food, he cuts my fingers, and breaks jests upon me. I bear them and beat him ; but by this light the dull-ey'd thinks he does well, does very well : but that he and I are of two faiths — I fill my belly and [he] feeds his brain — I could find in my heart to hug him — to hug him.

---

[1] See above, p. 3.
[2] *The Return from Parnassus*, I. 2.
[3] *Crites.* . . . If good Chrestus
Euthus, or Phronimus had spoke the words,
They would have moved me, and I should have called
My thoughts and actions to a strict account
Upon the hearing, etc.

The first part of this reminds us of the descriptions of Marston as Carlo Buffone, "a good feast-hound or banquet-beagle, that will scent you out a supper some three miles off,"[1] and as "Anaides of the ordinary."[2]

The beating which Quadratus gave Lampatho was perhaps what Jonson referred to when he told Drummond that he "beat" Marston.[3] "He and I are of two faiths," is a statement referring to the fact that Jonson was at that time a Roman Catholic.[4]

The stage war is clearly alluded to in the following passage: —

Quadratus. The Irish flux upon thy muse, thy whorish muse.
 Here is no place for her loose brothelry.
 We will not deal with her. Go! away, away!
Lampatho. I'll be revenged.
Quadratus. How, prithee? in a play? Come, come, be sociable.
 In private severance from society;
 Here leaps a vein of blood inflamed with love,
 Mounting to pleasure, all addict to mirth;
 Thou'lt read a satire or a sonnet now,
 Clogging their airy humour with —
Lampatho. Lamp-oil, watch-candles, rug-gowns, and small juice,
 Thin commons, four o'clock rising, — I renounce you all.
 Now may I 'ternally abandon meat,
 Rust, fusty, you which most embraced disuse.
 You ha' made me an ass; thus shaped my lot,
 I am a mere scholar, that is a mere sot.[5]

It is probable that the last words of Lampatho here are ironical, with allusion, however, to Jonson's well-known position as a scholar. Crites (Jonson) is said by Anaides (Marston) to

---

[1] "Character" of Carlo Buffone, prefixed to *Every Man out of his Humour*.
[2] *Cynthia's Revels*, I. 1.
[3] See *Jonson's Conversations with Drummond*, pp. 11, 20.
[4] See above, p. 124.
[5] IV. 1.

smell "all lamp-oil with studying by candle-light."[1] Rug gowns were worn, not only by scholars, but also by astrologers, and we have a record of Jonson's having officiated on one occasion in the latter capacity, for he told Drummond of an appointment which he made with "a lady . . . to meet ane old Astrologer, in the suburbs, . . . and it was himself disguysed in a longe gowne and a whyte beard at the light of dimm burning candles."[2] There are numerous allusions to Lampatho as a satirist, and also to Quadratus as being fond of wine. A probable reference to Jonson's physical size is Lampatho's statement (III, 2), "I'll make greatness quake: I'll taw the hide of thick-skin'd Hugeness," to which the following reply is made: —

> *Laverdure.*   'T is most gracious; we'll observe thee calmly.
> *Quadratus.*   Hang on thy tongue's end. Come on! prithee do.
> *Lampatho.*   I'll see you hanged first, I thank you, sir, I'll none.
> This is the strain that chokes the theatres;
> That makes them crack with full-stuff'd audience;
> This is your humour only in request,
> Forsooth to rail: this brings your ears to bed;
> This people gape for; for this some do stare.
> This some would hear to crack the author's neck.

It is probable that every time the word "hang" is used in connection with any representation of Jonson, there is an allusion to his narrow escape from the gallows.[3] There is in the lines of Lampatho a clear indication that the public took a keen interest in these satirical plays. Marston did not forget to ridicule Jonson's clothes, for at the beginning of the second act, when Quadratus is announced Laverdure says: —

> I'll not see him now, on my soul: he's in his old perpetuana suit.

---

[1] *Cynthia's Revels*, III. 2.
[2] *Jonson's Conversations with Drummond*, p. 21.
[3] See above, p. 7.

When Quadratus declares (II. 1), "Epithalamiums will I sing," we are reminded of the frequent allusion to Jonson's Epithalamiums in *Satiromastix*.[1] In the last act Quadratus is made to use "real," one of the "new-minted epithets" so ridiculed by Marston in *The Scourge of Villanie*,[2] and he promises to present in a play "a subject worth thy soul ; the honour'd end of Cato Utican." Mr. Fleay thinks, "possibly this is the play of *Cæsar and Pompey* afterwards finished by Chapman, but not acted."[3]

[1] See above, p. 120.
[2] See above, p. 8.
[3] *Chronicle of the English Drama*, II. 76.

XI.

THE RETURN FROM PARNASSUS AND TROILUS AND CRESSIDA.

IN our discussion up to this point we have found no evidence that Shakespeare was involved in "The War of the Theatres." *The Return from Parnassus*, a play "Publiquely acted by the students in Saint Johns Colledge in Cambridge" (as we are informed by the title-page of the quarto edition, 1606) contains one of the most interesting references to the quarrel of Marston and Jonson, for upon the passage have been founded many of the stories of the alleged enmity and quarrels of Ben Jonson and Shakespeare. *The Return from Parnassus* was performed at Christmastide, 1601–2, as is shown by internal evidence.[1]

---

[1] Professor Arber has reprinted the quarto edition (1606) of this play in *The English Scholar's Library*, No. 6. Prefixed to the text is a short discussion of the date at which the play was written. Professor Arber's results may be summarized as follows (references are to pages of the reprint): 1. The play is the last of a series of three plays by the same author (p. 5). 2. It was written and represented in Elizabeth's reign (p. 28). 3. It was written and represented subsequent to 11th August, 1600. On this date *Belvedere, or the Garden of the Muses*, the work attacked pp. 9, 10, was entered at the Stationers' Hall. 4. It was written for a Christmastide performance at St. John's College, Cambridge (pp. 4, 5, 42, 64, 66). As Queen Elizabeth died on the 24th March, 1603, we are of necessity shut up to a choice between the Christmastides of 1600-1, 1601-2, 1602-3. 5. Internal testimony establishes the writing of this play, for a first representation, in the Christmastide of 1601-2, 44 Eliz., possibly for a New Year's Day, which in 1602 (modern reckoning) fell on a Friday. The dominical letter is stated (p. 37) to have been C, which gives January 1, 1602, for the date. The dominical letter of 1601 was D, which explains the play upon the letters C and D in the reply of the Page to Sir Roderick (Act III. Sc. 1, p. 37), "C the Dominicall letter: it is true craft and cunning do so dominere; yet rather C and D are dominicall letters that is crafty Dunsery." 6. This date, 1601-2, is corroborated by the allusion to

We know, from the passage with which we are especially concerned, that the play as we have it was written after the performance of *Poetaster*, to which there is direct allusion. There is in the play much criticism of poets of the time, including Jonson and Marston, but with this we are not concerned. We are interested, however, in the following passage (IV. 3) :—

Kempe (to *Burbage*). Few of the university pen plaies well, they smell too much of that writer *Ovid*, and that writer *Metamorphosis*, and talke too much of *Proserpina* and *Juppiter*. Why heres our fellow *Shakespeare* puts them all downe, I and *Ben Jonson* too. O that *Ben Jonson* is a pestilent fellow, he brought up *Horace* giving the Poets a pill, but our fellow *Shakespeare* hath given him a purge that made him beray his credit.[1]

What was the "purge" given by Shakespeare to Ben Jonson? The natural answer is "a play." But, what play? The only play of Shakespeare's that it is at all possible to suppose was the "purge" is *Troilus and Cressida*, and there is

---

the siege of Ostend and the Irish Rebellion, both of which were at that time in progress (pp. 43, 50, 52). 7. This play was registered for publication at Stationers' Hall on the 16th October, 1605, and appeared in print with the date 1606. Mr. Fleay gives, in his *Chronicle of the English Drama*, II. 349-55, an interesting account of *The Return from Parnassus*, and an interpretation of the various characters. In regard to the date he says: "There is abundance of evidence in this play that fixes the date to 1601 or thereabouts" (p. 349). "The siege of Ostend had commenced, Nash was deceased, etc., — but the conclusive datum lies in the examination of Immerito, from which we learn that the dominical letter was C, and that the last quarter of the moon was on the fifth day at 2 h. 38 m. in the morning. This fixes the date as January, 1602–3, and if confirmation be needed we find it in what Momus says in the Prologue, 'What is here presented is an old musty show, that hath lain this twelvemonth in the bottom of a coal-house'" (p. 354). The statement of Momus may be taken as showing that the play, although written in 1601-2, was not acted until 1602-3. The dominical letter of 1603 was B, which does not accord with the statement in the play.

[1] The passage is given here as it is in the quarto, reprinted by Professor Arber. Professor Ward interprets the first mention of Ben Jonson's name as being in the nominative case. The context shows that it is an object of "puts down" and not a subject. Professor Ward's statement is: "The actor Kemp says — with some truth — that our fellow, Shakespeare, aye, and Ben Jonson too, puts down all the University play-writers." *A History of English Dramatic Literature*, II. 152.

evidence which seems to point to this play as in some way connected with the quarrel between Marston and Jonson. The sub-play in *Histriomastix* is *Troilus and Cressida*, in which occur the lines:—

> Thy knight his valiant elbow wears,
> That when he shakes his furious speare
> The foe in shivering fearful sort
> May lay him down in death to snort.[1]

In Shakespeare's *Troilus and Cressida* (I. 3) is the line :—

> When rank Thersites opes his mastic jaws.

The apparent play on Shakespeare's name in Marston's line coupled with the fact that it occurs in a parody of a play called *Troilus and Cressida* makes the line of Shakespeare seem a reply. That it is so is by no means certain, for Shakespeare's *Troilus and Cressida* is a play about the date of which there is considerable doubt. Henslowe mentions a play, by Dekker and Chettle, called "Troyeles and creasse daye,"[2] and this increases the difficulty of deciding whether Marston parodied Shakespeare's play. The play which Henslowe mentions has not come down to us.

---

[1] *Histriomastix*, II. 272-275.

[2] "Lent unto Thomas Downton, to lende unto Mr. Dickers and harey cheattell, in earneste of ther boocke called Troyeles and creasse daye, the some of iii£, aprell 7 daye 1599." *Henslowe's Diary*, p. 147.

"Lent unto harey cheattell and Mr. Dickers, in pte of payment of ther boocke called Troyelles and cresseda, xxs., the 16 of Aprell 1599." *Ibid.*, p. 148.

"Lent unto Mr. Dickers and Mr. Chettell, the 26 of maye 1599, in earneste of a Boocke called the tragedie of Agamemnon the some of xxxs." *Ibid.*, p. 153.

"Lent unto Robarte Shawe, the 30 of maye, 1599, in full paymente of the Boocke called the tragedie of Agamemnone, the some of iii£, vs., to Mr. Dickers and harey chettell." *Ibid.*, p. 153.

"The Tragedie of Agamemnon" is clearly the same play as "Troyeles and creasse daye." Collier says in his note that the title Agamemnon "is interlined over the words 'Troylles and creseda.'" *Ibid.*, p. 153.

As the present form of *Histriomastix* is of date 1599,[1] the parody of *Troilus and Cressida* which it contains may have reference to this play of Dekker and Chettle. If this is the case, there is no connection between the line of Marston and the line of Shakespeare. The assumption that there is a connection between the two lines has led to the conclusion that in Shakespeare's play Thersites is Marston, and since we are told that Shakespeare gave Ben Jonson a "purge," it has been concluded that Ajax is Jonson. Mr. Fleay supports the theory that *Troilus and Cressida* was the "purge," and says: —

> The "armed Prologue" [*Poetaster*] is very important. He appears in 'confidence,' and is unquestionably alluded to in the "armed Prologue" to *Troylus and Cressida*, who does not "come in confidence." It is then in this play of Shakespeare's that we must expect to find the purge that he gave to Jonson in return for the pill Jonson administered to Marston (cf. *Return from Parnassus*, IV. 3); and whoever will take the trouble to compare the description of Crites in *Cynthia's Revels* (II. 1) with that of Ajax in *Troylus and Cressida* (I. 2) will see that Ajax is Jonson: slow as the Elephant, crowded by Nature with "humors," valiant as the Lion, churlish as the Bear, melancholy without cause (compare Macilente). Hardly a word is spoken of or by Ajax in II. 3, III. 3, which does not apply literally to Jonson; and in II. 1 he beats Thersites of the "mastic jaws" (I. 3, 73. Histriomastix, Theriomastix) as Jonson "beat Marston" (*Drum. Conv.*, 11). Thersites in all respects resembles Marston, the railing satirist. But, it will be objected, *Troylus and Cressida* was not acted. It was not staled, indeed, on the London stage, but in 1601 the Chamberlain's men travelled and visited the Universities (see *Hamlet* in my *Life of Shakespeare*), and I have no doubt acted *Troylus and Cressida* at Cambridge, where the author of *The Return from Parnassus* saw it. The "purge" is from II. 3, 203, "he'll be the physician that should be the patient." When the Chamberlain's men returned to London at the close of 1601, Jonson, Marston, and Shakespeare were reconciled, and *Troylus* was not produced on the public stage.[2]

In this passage Mr. Fleay tries to prove that *Troilus and Cressida* was the "purge" by adducing proof that Ajax was

---

[1] See above, p. 32.   [2] *Chronicle of the English Drama*, I. 366.

Jonson. With the passage just quoted, compare the following statements by Mr. Fleay:—

> My hypothesis is that the "physic" given to "the great Myrmidon," I. 3, 378; III. 3, 34, is identical with the "purge" administered by Shakespeare to Jonson in *The Return from Parnassus*, IV. 3, and that the setting up of Ajax as a rival to Achilles shadows forth the putting forward Dekker by the King's men to write against Jonson his *Satiromastix*. The subsequent defection of Thersites from Ajax to Achilles would then agree with the reconciliation of Marston and Jonson in 1601, when they wrote together *Rosalind's Complaint*.[1]

In another passage Mr. Fleay says that Dekker is Thersites in *Troilus and Cressida*.[2]

In the first passage Mr. Fleay states that Ajax is Crites and therefore Jonson, Thersites is Marston; in the second passage, Ajax is Dekker, Achilles is Jonson, and Thersites is Marston; in the third passage Thersites is Dekker. Dr. Cartwright declares that "in *Troilus and Cressida* the character of Thersites, be it accidental or intentional, is an inimitable caricature of Crites and Horace, that is, of Jonson."[3] These contradictory statements by critics who advocate the theory that *Troilus and Cressida* was the "purge," are sufficient to awaken doubts, even though none had otherwise existed, as to the correctness of the theory. Were it not for the passage in *The Return from Parnassus*, it is not improbable that Shakespeare's name would not have been connected with the quarrel of Jonson, Marston, and Dekker. We have, however, the statement that Shake-

---

[1] *Chronicle of the English Drama*, II. 189.
[2] *ibid.*, I. 259.
[3] *Shakespeare and Jonson, Dramatic versus Wit Combats*, p. 13. The writer of an article entitled "Ben Jonson's Quarrel with Shakespeare" (*The North British Review*, July, 1870) states that "the reply to the *Poetaster* was *Troilus and Cressida*" (p. 420); that "Achilles is Jonson" (p. 421), and "Thersites is Dekker" (p. 422). The same critic calls attention (p. 424) to the interesting fact that in *Troilus and Cressida* Shakespeare uses many unusual words, evidently in defiance of Jonson's ridicule of Marston's words in *Poetaster*.

speare gave Jonson "a purge that made him beray his credit," and, for those who do not believe this to be a reference to *Troilus and Cressida*, and who fail to find Jonson satirized in any play of Shakespeare's, there remains a possible, but rather unsatisfactory solution of the difficulty. *Every Man in his Humour* and *Every Man out of his Humour* were first acted by the Chamberlain's company, the former at the Curtain, the latter at the Globe, which was built in 1599. Shakespeare was one of the actors who presented *Every Man in his Humour*, but, for some reason unknown to us, he did not act in *Every Man out of his Humour*, although the play was performed by the same company. The latter play contained Jonson's first attack on Marston, and was in every way more direct and bitter in its satirical representation of contemporaries,—a fact which may explain Shakespeare's taking no part. Jonson's connection with the Chamberlain's company then ceased, and his next two plays, *Cynthia's Revels* and *Poetaster*, were acted by the Chapel children. When Dekker's *Satiromastix*, voicing the general hostility to Jonson, was acted, it was by the Chamberlain's men at the Globe Theatre. This was by Shakespeare's company at Shakespeare's theatre, and therein may have consisted the giving of the "purge" to Jonson by Shakespeare.[1] The author of *The Return from Parnassus* makes no mention of *Satiromastix*, unless the latter play be after all the "purge." Gifford maintained that the "purge" was merely Shakespeare's great superiority to other playwrights. The "purge" must have been something more definite than this, and was presum-

---

[1] "The author of *The Return from Parnassus* could not have supposed that Shakespeare was the author of the *Satiromastix*; nor is his statement explained by the fact that that play was 'acted publicly by the Lord Chamberlain's servants,' even though we make the most improbable supposition that Shakespeare acted the part of William Rufus in it." *The North British Review*, July, 1870, p. 397. The explanation is not unreasonable, however, in spite of the opinion quoted.

ably a play. Dr. Brinsley Nicholson attempts to cut the knot by supposing the "purge" to have been some play of Shakespeare's which has not come down to us — a play, moreover, performed before *Poetaster*.[1] The latter statement is at variance with the evident meaning of the passage in *The Return from Parnassus*, while the supposition of a lost play is, at best, weak. This problem, like so many others concerning the Elizabethan drama, remains without any really satisfactory solution, and Shakespeare's connection with "The War of the Theatres" rests for proof wholly on the unexplained passage in *The Return from Parnassus*.

There have been numerous theories concerning Shakespeare's plays in this connection, and many of his characters have been identified by critics with Jonson, Marston, Dekker, and other contemporaries.[2] In no case has anything like sufficient proof been adduced in support of the theories.

---

[1] "It appears from *The Return from Parnassus* (IV. 3) that amongst the rest, the gentle Shakespeare, taking up the cause of his fellow dramatists, and perhaps also the interests of himself and his fellow actors, ridiculed him [Jonson] in some piece that has not come down to us, and, in the purge that he administered, gave Jonson the precedent for Horace's pills." *Ben Jonson*, ed. Brinsley Nicholson. Mermaid Series, I. 262.

[2] For a presentation of some of the various views of the relations of Shakespeare's plays to the quarrel, the reader is referred to *The North British Review*, July, 1870, "Ben Jonson's Quarrel with Shakespeare," and to Dr. Cartwright's monograph, *Shakespeare and Jonson, Dramatic versus Wit Combats*. A specimen of the kind of criticism by which Shakespeare has been involved in the stage war is the following passage of Dr. Cartwright's (p. 50): "We may take, as a secure basis or ground to build upon, Jonson's three 'Comical Satires,' as he calls them: *Every Man out of his Humour* was brought out in 1599; *Cynthia's Revels* in 1600; and the *Poetaster* in 1601. Shakespeare replies to the first in *Much Ado*, followed by *As You Like It;* about the same time Marston brings out the first and second parts of *Antonio and Mellida*. Shakespeare then, indignant at the fresh insults offered to himself and Lyly in the characters of Amorphus and Asotus, pours forth his wrath on Jonson as Apemanthus, and repays Marston for the travesty of *Hamlet* by painting him as the Athenian general Alcibiades, a brave soldier, but of dissolute morals. Marston retaliates on Shakespeare in the *Malcontent;*

and Jonson in the *Poetaster* takes his revenge on both of them. Marston replies again in the *Dutch Courtesan*, and Shakespeare repays both Jonson and Marston in *Othello* as well as in *Troilus and Cressida*." "Who can doubt that Iago is malignant Ben?" *Ibid.*, p. 28. Mr. Fleay says: "Shakespeare's *Twelfth Night or What You Will*, which introduces Malevole (Marston) as Malvolio, and addresses him in an anagrammatic way as M. O. A. I., *i.e.* Jo. Ma. (John Marston), I take to be his rejoinder to the two plays *What You Will* and *The Malcontent* in 1601-2." *Chronicle of the English Drama*, II. 77. "With the locking up of Crispinus [*Poetaster*] in some dark place, compare the imprisonment of Malvolio in *Twelfth Night*," *ibid.*, I. 369.

XII.

CONCLUSION.

In the preceding pages has been set forth the evidence showing that the plays discussed were connected with "The War of the Theatres." That these were the only plays concerned in the quarrel is by no means certain. It remains to be proved, however, that other plays were so involved, and in the absence of such proof the discussion has been confined to these fifteen plays. The purpose of the first of the accompanying tables is to exhibit the relationship of these plays as regards the order in which they were acted, the authors, theatres, and companies. The second table gives in summarized form both the proved and the conjectural identifications which have been mentioned in the discussion of individual plays.

TABLE No. I. — PLAYS.

In these tables conjectural matter is indicated by Italics.

PLAY.	DATE.	AUTHOR.	THEATRE.	COMPANY.
Every Man in his Humour	1598	Jonson	Curtain	Chamberlain's
The Case is Altered	1598 [1]	Jonson	Blackfriars'	Chapel children [2]
Histriomastix	1599	Marston [3]	*Curtain*	*Derby's* [4]
Every Man out of his Humour	1599	Jonson	Globe	Chamberlain's
Patient Grissil	1600	Dekker Chettle Haughton	Rose	Admiral's
Cynthia's Revels	1600	Jonson	Blackfriars'	Chapel children
Antonio and Mellida	1600	Marston	Paul's	Children of Paul's
Jack Drum's Entertainment	1600	Marston	Paul's	Children of Paul's
Antonio's Revenge	1600	Marston	Paul's	Children of Paul's
Poetaster	1601	Jonson	Blackfriars'	Chapel children
Satiromastix	1601	Dekker	Globe (publicly) Paul's (privately)	Chamberlain's Children of Paul's
What You Will	*1601*	Marston	*Blackfriars'* *Paul's*	*Chapel children* [5] *Children of Paul's*
Troilus and Cressida	*1601* [6]	Shakespeare	*at Cambridge,* [7] *Globe*	Chamberlain's
The Return from Parnassus	1601–2	?	at St. John's College, Cambridge	University players
The Spanish Tragedy	1602	(Kyd) Jonson	Fortune	Admiral's [8]

[1] *The Case is Altered* may have been performed before *Every Man in his Humour*, but we cannot prove it to have been.

[2] *The Case is Altered* " was performed by the children of the Queen's Revels at the Blackfriars'." *A History of English Dramatic Literature*, A. W. Ward, I. 557. Until 1604 this company was called the Chapel children.

[3] See above, p. 31.

[4] See above, p. 33, note 2.

[5] No company or theatre is mentioned on the title-page of the quarto, 1607. Mr. Fleay thinks it was acted by the Chapel boys, and that the date was 1601. *Chronicle of the English Drama*, II. 76. Mr. Bullen puts the date "shortly after the appearance of *Cynthia's Revels*." *Marston*, I. xlv. Marston's plays, which immediately preceded *What You Will*, were performed by the children of Paul's, and this play may have been performed by the same company.

[6] *Troilus and Cressida* as we have it seems to have been written at several different times, some of it being as late as 1606–7. The play has been discussed as being possibly the "purge" referred to in *The Return from Parnassus*, a play performed at Cambridge at Christmas, 1601–2 or 1602–3. If it is the "purge," which is at least doubtful, the reference must be to some performance after *Poetaster* and before *The Return from Parnassus*.

[7] *Chronicle of the English Drama*, Fleay, I. 366.

[8] See above, p. 99. Henslowe's company was the Admiral's, and they acted in 1601 at the Fortune Theatre.

TABLE No. II.—CHARACTERS.

Identifications which may be regarded as certain are in Roman type, and those which are doubtful or incorrect are in Italics. References are to pages on which the identifications are discussed.

THE SCOURGE OF VILLANIE.

Torquatus = Jonson (pp. 2, 6).

EVERY MAN IN HIS HUMOUR.

Master Mathew = Daniel (p. 24).
George Downright = *Jonson* (p. 19).
Master Stephen = *Shakespeare* (p. 17).
Wellbred = *Shakespeare* (p. 17).
Justice Clement = *Lyly* (p. 20).
Kitely = *Ford* (p. 21).
Cash = *Nashe* (p. 21).
Knowell = *Chapman* (p. 23).

THE CASE IS ALTERED.

Antonio Balladino = Monday (p. 37).

HISTRIOMASTIX.

Chrisoganus = Jonson (p. 33), *Marston* (p. 35).
Posthast = Monday (p. 38), *Shakespeare* (pp. 34, 42).
Sir Oliver Owlet's men = Pembroke's company (pp. 42, 116), *the Chamberlain's company* (pp. 34, 114).

EVERY MAN OUT OF HIS HUMOUR.

Asper-Macilente = Jonson (p. 57).
Carlo Buffone = Marston (p. 44), *Dekker* (p. 46, note 1).
Fastidious Brisk = Daniel (p. 52), *Dekker* (p. 46, note 1), *Lyly* (p. 52, note 1).
Fungoso = Lodge (p. 56).
Puntarvolo = Monday (pp. 64, 92), *Lyly* (p. 64, note 2), *Sir John Harington* (p. 64, note 2).
Deliro = *Monday* (p. 65, note 1; p. 110).
Clove = *Marston* (p. 51, note 1).
Orange = *Dekker* (p. 51, note 1).
Luculento = *Drayton* (p. 55, note 2), *Lord Berkeley* (p. 55).
Sogliardo = *a Burbadge* (p. 61, note 2), *Ralph Hogge* (p. 63).
Sordido = *a Burbadge* (p. 61, note 2), *Henslowe* (p. 62).

PATIENT GRISSIL.

Emulo = Daniel (p. 69), *Jonson* (p. 68).
Owen = *Lord Berkeley* (p. 70).

CYNTHIA'S REVELS.

Crites = Jonson (pp. 76, 96).
Anaides = Marston (p. 77), *Dekker* (p. 46, note 1; p. 79; p. 84, note 2).
Hedon = Daniel (pp. 76, 81), *Marston* (p. 84, note 2), *Dekker* (p. 84, note 2).

Asotus = Lodge (p. 85), *Lyly* (p. 150, note 2).
Amorphus = Monday (pp. 64, 90, note 1; 92), *Shakespeare* (p. 94, note 2; p. 150, note 2), *Lyly* (p. 119, note 4), *Barnaby Rich* (p. 90, note 3).

ANTONIO AND MELLIDA.

A Painter = Jonson (p. 98).

JACK DRUM'S ENTERTAINMENT.

Monsieur John fo de King = Jonson (p. 71).
Brabant Senior = *Jonson* (p. 72), *Hall* (p. 73).
Brabant Junior = *Marston* (p. 72).
Sir Edward Fortune = *Edward Alleyn* (p. 73).
Mammon = *Henslowe* (p. 73).
Timothy Tweedle = *Anthony Monday* (p. 75).
Christopher Flawn = *Christopher Beeston* (p. 75).
John Ellis = *John Lyly* (p. 75).
Planet = *Shakespeare* (p. 75).
Pasquil = *Nicholas Breton* (p. 75), *Nashe* (p. 75).

POETASTER.

Horace = Jonson (p. 107).
Crispinus = Marston (p. 107), *Dekker* (p. 107).
Demetrius = Dekker (pp. 79, 113).
Tigellius = *Daniel* (p. 109).
Tibullus = *Daniel* (p. 108).
Delia = *Elizabeth Carey* (p. 108).
Ovid = *Donne* (p. 108), *Shakespeare* (p. 108, note 4; p. 116, note 4).
Virgil = *Chapman* (p. 109), *Shakespeare* (p. 109).
Albius = *Monday* (p. 110).
Histrio = *an actor of Pembroke's company* (p. 116), *an actor of the Chamberlain's company* (p. 116).

SATIROMASTIX.

Horace = Jonson (p. 120).
Crispinus = Marston (p. 135).
Demetrius = Dekker (p. 120).
William Rufus = *Shakespeare* (p. 119, note 4).
Sir Vaughan ap Rees = *Lyly* (p. 119, note 4).

WHAT YOU WILL.

Quadratus = Jonson (p. 138), *Hall* (p. 138, note 2), *Marston* (p. 139, note 3).
Lampatho = Marston (p. 138).
Philomuse = *Daniel* (p. 137, note 3).

TROILUS AND CRESSIDA.

Ajax = *Jonson* (p. 147), *Dekker* (p. 148).
Achilles = *Jonson* (p. 148).
Thersites = *Jonson* (p. 148), *Marston* (p. 147), *Dekker* (p. 148).

INDEX.

Achilles, 148.
Actors, Memoirs of, 122.
acute, 91.
Admiral's company, 33, 68, 70.
Æneid, 106.
Æsop, 115.
Affaniae, 48.
Agamemnon, 146.
Albius, 65, 89, 110.
Alcibiades, 150.
ALLEYN, EDWARD, 73, 74.
Ambition, 82, 83.
American Journal of Philology, 34, 42.
Amores, 106.
Amorphus, 39, 63, 64, 76, 80, 81, 84–96, 99, 118, 120, 150.
Anaides, 39, 46, 50, 76–82, 84, 85, 94, 96, 99, 109, 111, 132, 141.
Antiquary, The, 14.
Antonio, see Balladino.
Antonio and Mellida, 1, 4, 74, 97, 98–101, 114, 116, 117, 135, 150.
Antonio's Revenge, 98, 114, 116, 117.
Apemanthus, 150.
Apologetical Dialogue, 2.
Apologie for Poetrie, 14.
ARBER, EDWARD, 14, 30, 93, 144, 145.
Arete, 78, 95, 96.
Argurion, 87, 88, 96.
ARIOSTO (tr.: Harington), 64.
Aristius, 110.
ARMIN, ROBERT, 137.
arride, 91.
Ars Poetica, 10.

As You Like It, 150.
Asinius Bubo, 119-122, 124, 126, 128, 129, 131.
Asinius Lupus, 119.
Asotus, 18, 19, 76, 82, 85–90, 92, 93, 150.
Asper, 19, 20, 57, 125.
Astræa, 33.
Astrophel and Stella, 25.
Athenæum, The, 7, 8.
ATKINS, W. H., 63.
At the Author's Going into Italy, 84.
Atticus, 137.
AUGUSTUS CÆSAR, 104, 106, 116.

Babulo, 70.
Balladino, Antonio, 37, 38, 91, 94.
barbarous, 82.
BAUDISSIN, WOLF, GRAF VON, 16.
belch, 36, 37.
Belvedere, or the Garden of the Muses, 144.
Ben Jonson's Quarrel with Shakespeare, 148, 150.
Ben Jonson und seine Schule, 16.
Berkeley, Lord and Lady, 55, 70.
Biancha, 14.
Bibliographers' Manual, 93.
Biographical Chronicle of the English Drama, see Fleay.
BIRDE, WILLIAM, 99.
Blirt, 137.
Boar's Head Tavern, 63.
Bobadil, 14, 22, 25, 59–61, 110.

Bobadilla, 14.
Booke of the Seven Planets, 118.
Brabant Junior, 72-74.
Brabant Senior, 71-74.
Brainworm, 14, 18, 22, 25, 60.
breeches, Pythagoricall, 120.
BRETON, NICHOLAS, 75.
Bridget, 14, 25, 27.
Brisk, Fastidious, 18, 44, 48-59, 65, 69, 70, 81, 82, 84, 91.
browne Ruscus, 4, 12.
Bubo, see Asinius.
Buffone, Carlo, 12, 44-53, 55, 56, 58, 61, 64, 68, 77-80, 94, 98, 125, 141.
BULLEN, A. H., 3-5, 7, 9, 12, 73, 85, 99, 138, 139.
BURBADGE, RICHARD, 61, 145.

Cæsar, see Augustus.
Cæsar and Pompey, 143.
Camden Society Publications, 120.
capreal, 51.
capricious, 69.
CAREY, ELIZABETH, 52, 55, 70, 108.
CAREY, GEORGE, 52.
Carlo, see Buffone.
CARTWRIGHT, ROBERT, 17, 20, 21, 47, 64, 85, 108, 120, 148, 150.
Case is Altered, The, 1, 31-43, 51, 58, 91, 92, 94, 95, 106.
Cash, Thomas, 14, 21, 25.
Cato Utican, 143.
Chamberlain's company, 33, 34, 42, 44, 61, 63, 77, 105, 114, 115, 119, 143, 147, 149.
Chapel children, 77, 99, 102, 119, 133, 149.
CHAPMAN, GEORGE, 14, 23, 28, 50, 74, 105, 109, 118.
CHESTER, ROBERT, 118.
CHETTLE, HENRY, 42, 46, 62, 68, 70, 74, 146.
Children of Paul's, 114, 115.
chirall, 138.

chival, 138.
Chloe, 65, 89, 110, 111.
Chrisoganus, 31-34, 101.
Chronicle of the English Drama, see Fleay.
CICERO, 6.
Cinedo, 48.
circumference, 51.
Citizen and his wife, 65, 77.
Civill Warres, 24.
Clement, 14, 20, 21, 28, 29.
Clout, 36.
Clove, 31, 50, 51, 69, 71, 118.
Cob, 14, 20, 22, 25.
Colin Clout, 24.
Collectanea Anglo-Poetica, 4, 48.
COLLIER, J. P., 14, 68, 99, 122, 146.
Commentaries on American Law, 105.
Comodey of Umers, 14.
Complaint of Rosamond, 53.
compliment, 69.
connive, 126.
CONSTABLE, HENRY, 30.
contemplation, 51.
Conversations with Drummond, Ben Jonson's, see Drummond.
Cordatus, 44, 45, 57, 65.
CORSER, REV. THOMAS, 4, 48.
Cos, 85.
Coxcomb, The, 50.
Criminal Law of England, History of the, 105.
Crispinus, 11, 35, 46, 71, 80, 106, 107, 109, 110-119, 121-123, 125, 126, 129, 130, 133, 135, 136, 138, 151.
Crites, 19, 76-79, 81, 83, 88, 89, 95-97, 125, 140, 141, 147.
Criticus, 19, 20, 125.
CUMBERLAND, ANNE, COUNTESS OF, 54, 55.
CUMBERLAND, MARGARET, COUNTESS OF, 54.
CUNNINGHAM, PETER, 21.
Curtain theatre, 149.

Cutpurse, Moll, 12.
Cynthia's Revels, 1, 5, 9, 18, 19, 39, 46, 50, 63-65, 74, 76-97, 99-101, 110, 111, 115, 117, 118, 120, 125-128, 130-132, 134, 136, 140, 141, 147, 150.

DANIEL, JOHN, 109.
DANIEL, SAMUEL, praise of, by Marston, one of the causes of the "War," 6; reason suggested for Jonson's hostility towards, 13, 24, 82, 96; satirized by Jonson, as Mathew, Brisk, and Hedon (q.v.), 19; poetry of, satirized by Jonson, Davies, and, according to Fleay, by Shakespeare, 24-30, 53, 54; as Emulo (q.v.), 51; facts in the life of, 54, 82; intimates in *Delia* that he has been wronged, 55; imitated and praised by Lodge, 56; as Musus, 74; called a "poet in the court account" by Jonson, 82; plagiarism of, 83; referred to in Envy prologue to *Poetaster*, 84; not Ovid or Tibullus, 108; possibly Hermogenes Tigellius, 109; relation of John Daniel to. 109: as Philemon, 137.
Daniel, Works of Samuel (ed. Grosart), 83.
DAVIES, SIR JOHN, 54, 74, 89, 109.
Davies, Poems of Sir John, 54, 75, 89.
Decius, 74.
Defence of Contraries, The. 92.
De Finibus, 6.
Deformed, one, 94.
DEKKER, THOMAS, quarrel of, with Jonson, 1; reference to the *Troilus and Cressida* of, and Chettle, 42, 146; not Carlo Buffone or Anaides, 46, 79, 84, 85; not Orange, 51; connection of, with the "War," 46, 51, 67, 68, 70, 107, 113, 120; not Fastidious Brisk, 47; "hired" to attack Jonson in *Satiromastix*, 67, 105, 114, 119,

148; first satirized by Jonson as Demetrius (q.v.), 67; participation of, in *Patient Grissil*, 68, 70; collaborates with Jonson, 68; *Guls Hornebooke* of, quoted, 69, 111; appropriates to himself lines of Jonson which referred to others, 80; not Hedon, 85; possibly referred to in the phrase "these libels" in *Poetaster*, 103; possibly one of the "better natures" referred to in *Poetaster*, 105; not Crispinus, 107; refers to Jonson's allusions to Marston in *Poetaster*, 111; parodies Jonson's pun on Crispinus, 112; a rapid writer and a "dresser of plays," 114, 119, 121; boast of, concerning the *Seven Deadly Sins*, 114; at work upon a play upon the story of Sir Walter Terill, 119; probably had a real admiration of Jonson, 120; offended by the reference to the "Moor," 133; shows magnanimity in his attitude towards Jonson, 134; not Ajax, 148; not Thersites, 148.
Dekker, Works of Thomas (Grosart), 70, 112; (Pearson), 22, 76, 80, 112.
Delia, 24, 29, 30, 53, 56, 70, 82-84, 108.
Deliro, 49, 55, 56, 58, 59, 64, 65, 89, 110.
Delphicke, 4, 5, 8-10, 50.
Demetrius, 46, 68, 76, 79, 80, 105-108, 110, 113, 114, 116-118; (in *Satiromastix*), 119-121, 127, 129, 130, 133, 136.
demonstrate, 51.
Derby's company, 33, 42.
Desmond, Ode to, 10.
detraction, 79, 80.
Diary, see Henslowe, Manningham.
Dicaee, 123.
Dictionary of National Biography, 21, 52, 55, 62, 85, 86, 88, 92.
die-note, long, 84, 93.
Diogenicall, 51.

Discourse of English Poetrie, 93.
Discourse of Poesie (Jonson), 24.
DODSLEY, ROBERT, *Old English Plays*, 100.
Dogberry, 94.
Dominical letter, 144.
DONNE, JOHN, 108.
Doricus, 137.
Downright, George, 14, 18, 19, 23, 24, 26, 28, 29, 60.
DOWNTON, THOMAS, 146.
DRAKE, NATHAN, 107.
Dramatic Literature, A History of English, 109, 138, 145.
Dramatick Poets, English, 31, 107.
DRAYTON, MICHAEL, 56, 74, 89, 110, 118.
DRUMMOND OF HAWTHORNDEN, WILLIAM, 2, 6-8, 10, 12, 24, 35, 39, 40, 41, 71, 72, 79, 82, 102, 105, 107, 113, 123, 141, 142, 147.
duel, Jonson's, 7, 8, 68, 71, 122, 124, 142.
Dutch Courtezan, 151.
DYCE, ALEXANDER, 16.

Early London Theatres, 105.
Eastward Ho, 105, 118.
Echo, 131.
ecliptic, 51.
ELIZABETH, QUEEN, 31, 33, 53, 87.
Ellis, John, 75.
eloquence, dumb, 53, 54.
Emulo, 51, 55, 68-70, 121.
Endimion and Phœbe, 74.
English Dramatic Literature, A History of, 109, 138, 145.
English Dramatick Poets, 31, 107.
English Poets and Poesy, 24, 38.
English Romayne Life, The, 92.
Envy, 84, 134.
Epigrammata (Martial), 103, 106.
Epigrams, 59, 111; (Jonson), 120, 133, 134.

Epistle to Elizabeth, Countess of Rutland, 82.
Epithalamiums, Jonson's, 120, 143.
epithets, new-minted, 4-11, 32, 50, 51, 91, 117.
Euphues and his England, 20.
Every Man in His Humour, 1, 9, 13-30, 34, 35, 38, 44, 53, 58, 60, 61, 77, 79, 108, 115, 125, 149, 150.
Every Man Out of His Humour, 1, 5, 9, 18-20, 22, 25, 32, 34, 35, 38-40, 44-66, 69, 70, 71, 73, 76-78, 80, 82, 85, 89, 90-94, 98, 100, 108-110, 112, 115, 118, 119, 125, 126, 134, 141, 149, 150.
Faery Queen, 22.
Fallace, 55, 59, 65, 89, 110.
Fantasy of the passion of ye fox, 9.
Farneze, 69, 106.
fastidious, 69, 70.
fatuate, 117.
Faustus, 16.
Fig for Momus, A, 47, 56, 57, 89.
fist, late perfumed, 3, 8.
FITZGEFFREY, CHARLES, 48.
Flawn, Christopher, 75.
FLEAY, F. G. (*Chronicle of the English Drama*), 5-7, 14, 21, 32, 33, 40-43, 46, 53-56, 61, 64, 65, 69, 70, 73, 75, 79, 83, 89, 90, 94, 99, 100, 103, 108-110, 116, 117, 127, 133, 137, 143, 145, 147, 148, 151; (*History of the Stage*), 42, 116; (*Life of Shakespeare*), 147; (*Shakespeare Manual*), 61, 67, 112.
FLETCHER, JOHN, 50.
FORD, JOHN, 21.
Formal, 14.
Fortunatus, 33.
Fortune, Sir Edward, 73.
Fortune Theatre, 73, 116.
Fugitive Tracts, 10.
Fungoso, 18, 19, 55, 56, 65, 85, 87, 89, 108.
furibund, 117.

INDEX.

FURNIVALL, F. J., 10.
Fuscus, 110.
fustian, 50, 69, 71, 91, 118, 138, (cf. 11, 31).

gallimaufry of language, 68, 69.
Gallus, 109.
games in *Cynthia's Revels*, 77, 80, 95.
GASCOIGNE, GEORGE, 47.
GELLIUS, AULUS, 110.
Genealogist, The, 62.
Geronymo, 99.
GIFFORD, WILLIAM, 4, 8, 14, 22, 66, 107, 109, 111, 116, 126, 149.
Giulliano, 14.
Globe Theatre, 114–116, 149.
Golde, 89.
GOSSE, E. W., 56.
GOSSON, STEPHEN, 87.
GREENE, ROBERT, 16, 94.
GROSART, A. B., 4, 5, 11, 12, 16, 20, 24, 38, 54, 70, 75, 83, 89, 99, 108, 109, 112, 113.
Gulch, 36.
Guls Horne-booke, 69, 111.

HAKE, EDWARD, 47.
HALL, JOSEPH, 3, 4, 20, 21, 47, 48, 73, 74, 138.
HALLIWELL-PHILLIPPS, J. O., 4, 7, 11, 71, 93, 100, 106.
Hamlet, 150.
hang, 142.
Hannam, Horace, 22.
Harleian Miscellany, 92.
HARINGTON, SIR JOHN, 64, 89.
HASLEWOOD, JOSEPH, 24, 38.
HAUGHTON, WILLIAM, 68.
Have with you to Saffron Walden, 20.
HAYWOOD, JOHN, 89.
HAZLITT, W. C., 14, 100.
healths drunk kneeling, 50, 77, 78.
Hedon, 18, 76–85, 87, 91, 93, 96, 99, 109.

Henry IV., 42.
Henry V., 16, 42.
Henry VI., 16.
HENSLOWE, PHILIP, 14, 33, 37, 46, 56, 62, 63, 68, 73, 99, 100, 114, 146.
Henslowe, Philip, 62.
HERBERT, WILLIAM, 54.
HERFORD, C. H., 23, 84, 85, 109.
Hermogenes, see Tigellius.
Hero and Leander, 28.
Hesperida, 14, 53.
Hieronimo, 99, 123, 124.
History of English Dramatic Literature, A, 109, 138, 145.
History of the Stage, 42, 116.
Histrio, 31–43, 105, 110, 111, 114–116, 147.
Histriomastix, 1, 13, 31–44, 50, 51, 71, 94, 115, 146, 147.
HOGGE, RALPH, 63.
Honour, 82.
HORACE, 10, 102, 106, 110.
Horace, 19, 20, 22, 35, 68, 79, 104–107, 109–114, 116–118, 119; (*Satiromastix*), 119–136.
Hue and Cry after Cupid, The, 120.
humorous, 125.
Humorous Day's Mirth, A, 14.
humours, 125.
Hunterian Club Reprint, 87, 89.
HUTH, HENRY, 10.
Hymen, The Masque of, 120.

Idea, 74.
If I freely may discover, 106.
Immerito, 145.
In Dacum, 54.
In Decium, 75.
inflate, 117.
In Gallum, 109.
ingenious, 9.
ingenuity, 51.
INGLEBY, C. M., 62.
In Haywodum, 89.

intellectual, 51.
intrinsecate, 4, 5, 8-10, 50, 91.
Irish Rebellion, 145.
Italy, travels of Daniel and Monday in, 84, 89.

Jack Drum's Entertainment, 1, 40, 41, 67, 71-75, 78, 114, 116, 117.
Jeronimo, 22.
JONSON, BENJAMIN, quarrel with Marston, 1, 2, 4, 31, 32, 39, 45, 67, 71, 72, 113, 141, 144, 146; with Dekker, 1, 2, 4; as Torquatus (q.v.), 2; accused of "venerie," 2, 4, 40, 78; use of "new-minted epithets" by, 4-11, 32, 50, 51, 91, 117, 143; *opima spolia* taken by, 7, 123; duel and trial of, 7, 8, 68, 71, 122, 124, 142; "neck-verse" of, 7, 121, 122; branded, 7, 8; translation of *Ars Poetica* by, 10; ridicules Marston's diction, 11, 31, 32, 50, 67, 71, 91, 98, 117, 148; admiration of, for "Somerset," 11; dislike of, for Daniel, 13, 24, 82, 96; relations of, with Henslowe, 14, 99; views of, on the function of dramatic representation, 17; not Knowell, 17; not Downright, 19; as Asper, Crites, and Horace (q.v.), 19; career of, not alluded to in Brainworm, 22; relations of, with his step-father possibly shadowed forth in *Every Man in His Humour*, 23; no friend of Daniel's verse, 24-30, 53, 54; as Chrisoganus (q.v.), 31-44; allusions of, to his poverty, 35, 107; his arrogance, 35, 107, 135; his translations, 35; shows Marston how to write, 39; as John fo de King, 40, 41, 71; and Dekker, 46, 67, 68; as Macilente (q.v.), 57; shabby clothes of, 58, 77, 96, 129, 142; "rocky face" and "mountain belly" of, 59, 123, 142; characters of, usually persons, 66; not Emulo, 68, 69; collaborates with Dekker, 68; possible reference to duel and bricklaying of, 68, 120, 121; suggested identification of Brabant Senior with, 72; allusions to the scholarship of, 77, 96, 129, 141; pedantry of, 81; and Monday, 81, 92; and Lodge, 88; makes use of quarrel of Marston and Monday, 94, 96; finds it difficult to get money on his works, 96; scene of Marston's suggests a scene to, 98, 101; as "a Painter," 98; the word "limn" of, ridiculed by Marston, 99; on a more friendly footing with Marston, 100, 118, 137, 147; ridicules soldiers and lawyers and is brought before the Lord Chief Justice, 102, 108, 132, 134; personal attacks in the early comedies of, 102; refers to "libels" upon him, 103; legal difficulties of, because of his plays, 105; learning of, shown in *Poetaster*, 106; and Shakespeare, 108, 109, 116, 144; possibly Davies's Gallus, 109; references of, to Marston in the *Epigrams*, 111; ridicules Marston's coat of arms, 112; calls Dekker a "dresser of plays," 114, 119, 121; exonerates Marston from having had a share in *Satiromastix*, 114; last attack of, on Marston, 116; end of "War" for, 118; joins with Marston in writing plays, 118; *Malcontent* dedicated to, 118; Dekker's admiration for the really good qualities of, 120; references in the *Satiromastix* to the *Epigrams* and *Epithalamiums* of, 120; career of, as an actor referred to in *Satiromastix*, 123; religion of, referred to, 124, 141; relation of the plays of, to the times, 125; slowness of, in writing his plays, 130; suggested identification of, with Malevole, 137; possibly the "envious

hand" in *What You Will*, 138; as
Quadratus (q.v.), 138; suggested
identification of, with Lampatho, 139;
plays the astrologer, 142; Marston,
Shakespeare, and, reconciled, 147;
suggested identification of, with Ajax
(q.v.), 147; personal traits of, possibly referred to, 147; suggested identification of, with Achilles and Thersites (q.v.), 148; a "pestilent fellow,"
148; suggested identification of, with
Apemanthus (q.v.), 150; Cartwright's
view of the connection of, with the
"War," 150; suggested identification
of, with Iago, 151.
Jonson, *Essay on the Life and Dramatic
Writings of Ben*, 16.
Jonson, *Notes on the Conversations of Ben*,
see Drummond.
Jonson's *Quarrel with Shakespeare*, 148,
150.
Jonson *und seine Schule*, Ben, 16.
Jonson, *Mermaid edition of Ben*, 23, 51,
84, 109, 150.
Jonson, *Works of Ben* (Gifford), 4, 8,
22, 107, 109; (Whalley), 104.
Julia, 108, 116.
JUVENAL, 4, 106.

Kempe, 145.
KENT, JAMES, 105.
Kind Hartes Dreame, 62.
King, John fo de, 40, 41, 71, 72.
King Lear, 16.
Kinsayder, Don, 139, 140.
"Kinsayder, W.," 4.
Kiss, The, 84, 93.
Kitely, 14, 21, 23, 25.
Kitely, Dame, 14, 27.
Knowell, 14, 18, 22, 23, 25, 30.
Knowell, Edward, 14, 17, 18, 20, 23, 25-
27, 30, 108.
KYD, THOMAS, 99.

LABERIUS DECIMUS, 110.
LAING, DAVID, see Drummond.
LAMBERTON, W. A., 10.
Lampatho, 138-142.
Lancaster, 15, 16.
Landulpho, 43.
LANGBAINE, WILLIAM, 31, 107.
*Lascivious Knight and Lady Nature,
The*, 42.
Laureo, 70.
law and lawyers, Jonson's attack on,
102, 108, 132, 134.
Laverdure, 142.
LEE, SIDNEY, 52, 88.
Legend of Robert, Duke of Normandy,
110.
Lenten Stuffe, 38.
letter, Dominical, 144.
Lexiphanes, 106, 117.
libel and slander, laws regarding, 105.
libels, 103, 105.
*Life and Death of Captain Thomas
Stukeley, The*, 16, 133.
limn, 98.
Locrine, 16.
Lodge, *Memoir of Thomas* (Gosse), 56.
Lodge, *Thomas* (Lee), 88.
LODGE, SIR THOMAS, 85-87.
Lodge, *Sir Thomas* (Welch), 86.
LODGE, THOMAS, as Asotus and Fun-
goso (q.v.), 19; Daniel popular with,
and other critics, 24; "censured" in
Every Man in His Humour, 30; a
satirist before Hall, 47; fled beyond
seas from his tailor, 56; imitates and
praises Daniel, 57; referred to in
Satiromastix, 76; the father of, 85-
87; the fortunes of, referred to in
Cynthia's Revels, 87; a physician, 88;
personal appearance described, 88;
a Jack-of-all-trades, 88; *The Defence
of Contraries* attributed to, 93.
Lodge, *Works of Thomas* (Hunterian
Club), 56.

London Past and Present, 21.
London Prodigal, The, 59.
Looking Glass for London and England, A, 16.
Lorenzo Junior, 9, 14.
Lorenzo Senior, 14.
Love's Martyr, 118.
LOWNDES, W. T., 93.
LOYD, W. H., 105.
LUCIAN, 106.
Luculento, 55, 70.
LYLY, JOHN, 20, 21, 23, 52, 64, 75, 120, 150.

Macbeth, 16.
Maciliente, 25, 39, 45, 48-51, 53-55, 57-59, 62, 64, 65, 93, 101, 103.
Mahomet, 133.
Malcontent, 137, 150, 151.
Malevole, 137, 151.
Malvolio, 151.
Mammon, 72-74.
MANNINGHAM, JOHN, 120.
Manlius, Titus, 6-8.
MARLOWE, CHRISTOPHER, 12, 28.
MARSTON, JOHN, satires of, 1-12, 47, 48; quarrel of, with Jonson, 1, 2, 4, 31, 32, 39, 45, 67, 68, 71, 72, 113, 147; accuses Jonson of "venerie," 24, 40, 78; ridicules Jonson's "new-minted epithets," 4-11, 32, 50, 51, 91-117, 143; diction of, ridiculed by Jonson, 11, 31, 32, 50, 69, 71, 91, 98, 117, 148; relation of, to the authorship of *Histriomastix*, 31, 32; represents Jonson possibly as Chrisoganus, 31-33; possibly himself Chrisoganus, 34, 35; and Monday, 38, 39, 94, 96; as Carlo and as Anaides (q.v.), 39; shown by Jonson how to write, 39; as the "Grand Scourge or Second Untruss," 46, 48, 64, 105, 114, 117, 118; a gentleman by birth, 49, 111, 112; not Clove (q.v.), 51; the author of *Jack Drum's Entertainment*, 71; probably represented Jonson as John fo de King, 71; as Mellidus, 74; as Crispinus (q.v.), 80; frequent use of the word "guts" by, 81; assumed wrongly to be Hedon, 84, 85; ridicules Jonson's word "limn," 98; suggestion that a scene of Jonson's was parodied by, 99; age of, when matriculated at Oxford, 99; on better terms with Jonson, 100, 118, 137, 147, 148; in difficulties because of *Eastward Ho*, 105, 118; and the study of the law, 108; hair of, ridiculed, 111; Dekker refers to Jonson's allusions to, in *Poetaster*, 111; gentle birth of, referred to, 111, 112; coat of arms of, ridiculed, 112, 113; exonerated by Jonson from having had a share in *Satiromastix*, 114; last attack of Jonson on, 116; joins with Jonson in writing plays and dedicates *Malcontent* to him, 118, 138; *Satiromastix* written at the instigation of, and of others, 119; resented being called a "gentleman parcel-poet," 131; as Lampatho, 138; suggested identification of, with Quadratus, 139; reference in Troilus to, 147; reconciliation of Jonson, Shakespeare, and, 147; as Thersites, 148; connection of, with the "War," according to Cartwright, 150.
Marston, Poems of John (Grosart), 4, 5, 11, 12, 108, 113.
Marston, Works of John (Halliwell-Phillipps), 4, 7, 11; (Bullen), 4, 5, 7, 9, 12, 73, 85, 99, 138, 139.
MARTIAL, 103, 106.
Martin, 21.
Martin Marprelate controversy, 21, 105.
MARTIN, RICHARD, 102.
mathematical, 51.
Matheo, 14, 29.

Mathew, 14, 18, 19, 20, 23, 24, 25-30, 44, 79, 81, 83.
Mavortius, 34, 36.
May Day, 50.
Mellidus, 74.
Memoirs of Actors, 122.
Mercury, 77, 86, 91, 95, 97.
MERES, FRANCIS, 24, 38.
Merry Wives of Windsor, 42.
Metamorphosis of Ajax, 89.
Metamorphosis of Pigmalion's Image and Certaine Satyres, 5, 12, 47, 116.
Metheglin, 120.
Mew, 137.
MIDDLETON, THOMAS, 137.
Miniver, 123.
Minos, 110, 133.
Misprision, 69.
Mitis, 50, 57, 65, 66.
Momus, 145.
MONDAY, ANTHONY, as Antonio Balladino (q.v.), 37; pageant poet, 38, 81, 94, 95; probably Posthast (q.v.), 39; as Puntarvolo and Amorphus (q.v.), 39; a "gentleman scholar," 43; hissed off the stage for his singing, 43; as Deliro (q.v.), 65; suggested identification of Timothy Tweedle with, 75; relation of, to Marston, Daniel, and Lodge, 76; translations of, 90; uses "stale stuff," 91, 95; travels of, 92; *The Defence of Contraries* of, 92; songs of, 93, 94; and Marston, 94; reason for Jonson's satire of, 96; as Albius (q.v.), 110.
MONTAGUE, ANTHONY, VISCOUNT, 62.
Moor, the, 133.
MOORE, ANNE, 108.
Moria, 80, 111, 126.
Morphides, 118.
Morus, 87.
Mucedorus, 16, 101, 138.
Much Ado About Nothing, 94, 150.
Musco, 14, 28.

Musophilus, 137.
Musus, 74.
My Picture left in Scotland, 59, 123.
Myrmidon, the great, 148.

NASHE, THOMAS, 20, 21, 24, 38, 53, 75, 94, 145.
Nashe, Works of Thomas (Grosart), 24.
Nasutus, 103.
National Biography, Dictionary of, see Dictionary.
natures, better, 104.
neck-verse, 7, 121, 122.
Newes out of Paules Churchyarde, 47.
new-minted epithets, 4-11, 30, 50, 51, 91, 117, 143.
NICHOLSON, BRINSLEY, 1, 12, 14, 23, 51, 71, 84, 112, 113, 150.
North British Review, The, 69, 94, 137, 148-150.
Notes and Queries, 10, 71, 113.
NOTTINGHAM, EARL OF, 68.
oblatrant, 117.
obstupefact, 117.
Ode to Desmond, 10.
Of his Lady's not coming to London, 118.
O happy golden age!, 30.
Old English Plays, 100.
Old Fortunatus, 67, 68.
Onion, 37, 106.
optic, 91.
Orange, 31, 50, 51, 71.
ORDISH, T. F., 106.
Oseas, 16.
Ostend, siege of, 145.
O tears, no tears, 25.
Othello, 151.
Outlines of the Life of Shakespeare, 106.
OVID, 103, 104, 106, 121.
Ovid Junior, 23, 104, 108, 116.
Ovid Senior, 23.
Owen, 55, 68, 70.
Owlet's Company, Sir Oliver, 33, 34, 42, 115, 116.

INDEX.

Page, the, 144.
"pagge of plimothe," 68.
Palinode, the, 126.
Palladis Tamia, 24, 38.
PALMER, SIR HENRY, 87.
Parasitaster, 137.
parcel-poet, 111, 131.
Pasquil, 73, 75.
Patient Grissil, 1, 16, 51, 56, 67-70.
PAVIER, T., 100.
PEELE, GEORGE, 32.
Peele, Works of George (Dyce), 16.
Pembroke, Mary, Countess of, 54, 55.
Pembroke's company, 92, 116.
PERRY, G. G., 21.
PERSIUS, 4.
Peto, 14.
Phantaste, 88, 90.
Philarchus, 34.
Philargyrus, 85, 86.
Philautia, 81, 82, 83, 88, 91.
Phillis, 24.
Phillis Honoured with Pastoral Sonnets, 56, 87.
Philomuse, 137.
Piers Pennilesse, 24.
pill, emetic, 11, 106, 117, 136, 145, 147.
Pizo, 14.
Planet, 73-75.
Playwright, epigrams of Jonson on, 111, 120.
Plays Confuted in Five Actions, 87.
Plays, Dictionary of Old, 100.
Plays, Old English, 100.
Poet-Ape, epigrams of Jonson on, 120, 133, 134.
Poetaster, 1, 2, 4, 11, 22, 35, 39, 46, 65, 67, 68, 71, 79, 84, 89, 91, 98, 100-123, 125, 126, 128-134, 136, 137, 145, 148, 150, 151.
polite, 91.
Political Use of the Stage, The, 94.
Polyposus, 103, 105.
pommado, 11, 82.

Posthast, 34, 37, 38, 41-43, 94.
Practise (Saviolo), 90.
Privy Council, Register of the, 105.
Prodigal Child, The, 32, 42.
projects, 69.
Prologue, armed, 147.
Promos and Cassandra, 14.
prorumped, 117.
Prosaites, 85, 86.
Prospero, 14, 29.
Puntarvolo, 39, 46, 48-50, 80, 90, 92, 94.
purge, 104, 145-150.
Pyrgi, the, 110, 115, 116, 123, 133, 147.
Pythagoran, 51.
Pythagorical, 51, 91.
Pythagoricall breeches, 120.

Quadratus, 138-143.
Quintilian, Sir, 123.

RACSTER, JOHN, 118.
Ramnusia's whippe, 35.
RANKINS, WILLIAM, 47.
reall, 4, 5, 8-10, 50, 143.
Rebellion, Irish, 145.
reciprocal, 91, 118.
reciprocally, 91.
Register of the Privy Council, 105.
RENDLE, WILLIAM, 62.
retrograde, 91, 117, 118.
Return from Parnassus, The, 1, 30, 90, 104, 144-151.
rhetoric, sweet silent, 53, 54.
RICH, BARNABY, 64, 90.
Richard Crookback, 37, 99.
Robart the second, Kinge of Scottes Tragedie, 68.
Robert, Duke of Normandy, Legend of, 110.
Roderick, Sir, 144.
Romeo and Juliet, 116.
Rosalind's Complaint, 148.
Rosamond, 24.
Rose, the, 70.

INDEX.

Rowland, 89.
Rufus, William, 119, 125, 134, 135, 149.
rug gown, 129, 142.
Ruscus, browne, 4, 12.
RUTLAND, ELIZABETH, COUNTESS OF, 24, 82.

St. Bartholomew the Less, Parish of, 21.
St. John's College, 144.
St. Saviour, Parish of, 62.
Satiræ, 102, 106, 110.
Satires, 1–12, 47, 48, 73, 74, 110.
Satiro, 19.
Satiromastix, 1, 35, 51, 67, 76, 80, 81, 103, 107, 112, 114, 117, 118–136, 143, 147.
Saviolina, 53.
SAVIOLO, 90.
SCHELLING, F. E., 10.
SCHMIDT, ALEXANDER, 16.
School of Shakspere, The, 15, 16, 31, 32, 85, 116.
Scourge, Grand, 46, 48, 64.
Scourge of Villanie, The, 2–6, 8, 9, 11, 31, 32, 35, 46–48, 50, 51, 79, 91, 116, 117, 143.
SECCOMBE, THOMAS, 92.
Seven Deadly Sins of London, The, 114.
Seven Planets, Booke of the, 118.
Seven Satyres applied to the Week, 47.
Shakespeare and Jonson, Dramatic versus Wit Combats, etc., see Cartwright.
Shakespeare Burlesqued by Two Fellow Dramatists, 34, 42.
Shakespeare, Life of (Halliwell-Phillipps), 106; (Fleay), 147.
Shakespeare Manual, 61, 67, 112.
Shakespeare's Library, 14.
Shakespeare Society Publications, 68, 122; (*Transactions of the New*), 62, 94.
SHAKESPEARE, WILLIAM, and the "War," 1, 17, 144–151; not criticised necessarily in the Prologue to *Every Man in His Humour*, 14–16; not Stephen or Wellbred, 17; Jonson second only to, 33; suggested identification of Posthast with, 34, 41–43; suggested reference by, to Daniel, 54; suggested identification of Planet with, 75; suggestion that the nickname "Deformed" was applied by his critics to, 94; possibly one of the "better natures," 104; and Jonson, 108, 109, 116, 144, 150; suggested identification of, with Ovid, 108; with Virgil, 109; identified by critics with at least one character in every play, 119; suggested identification of, with William Rufus, 119, 120; story that Jonson's release after his duel was due to the intervention of, 122; "puts down" all the University playwrights, 145; the "purge" of, 145–150; Jonson, Marston, and, reconciled, 147.
Shakspere and his Time, 107.
Shakspere Allusion-Books, 62.
Shakspere, School of, see Simpson.
SHAWE, ROBERT, 146.
Shift, 59, 60, 104, 120.
Shoemaker's Holiday, The, 33, 67, 68.
SIDNEY, PHILIP, SIR, 14, 25, 54.
Siege of Ostend, 145.
Silence, Justice, 89.
SIMPSON, RICHARD, 15, 16, 31, 32, 34–37, 40, 42, 43, 51, 71, 72, 74, 85, 94, 116.
sintheresis, 69.
Sir Clyomon and Clamydes, 16.
SMITH, HOMER, 30.
Snuff, 137.
Sogliardo, 12, 19, 45, 49, 58, 60–62, 93, 112.
Somerset, 11.
Sordido, 61, 62, 73.
Southwark, 62, 63.
Spanish Invasion, 33.
Spanish Tragedy, The, 22, 23, 25, 99–101.

168   INDEX.

SPENCER, GABRIEL, 68, 121.
SPENSER, EDMUND, 22, 24, 54.
Spenser, Works of Edmund (Grosart), 24.
spurious, 117.
State Papers, 87.
Stationers' Register, 8, 90, 144.
Steel Glass, The, 47.
Stephano, 14.
Stephen, 14, 17-19, 26, 60, 61.
STEPHENS, SIR JAMES, 105.
STEWART, LADY FRANCES, 120.
Stukeley, The Life and Death of Captain Thomas, 16, 133.
substantives and adjectives, game of, 80, 82, 91.
synderisis, 51, 69.

Tempest, The, 16.
Terill, Sir Walter, 119.
Terrours of the Night, The, 53.
Theatres, Early London, 105.
Theriomastix, 147.
Thersites, 146-148.
thing done and who did it. game of, a, 77, 95.
THOMPSON, W., 63.
Thorello, 14.
Tib, 14.
Tibullus, 108.
Tigellius, Hermogenes, 106, 108-110.
Timber, Jonson's, 10.
Torquatus, 2-11, 48.
traveller, 95.
Trebatius, 102.
Troilus and Cressida (Shakespeare), 1, 42, 101, 144-151; (sub-play in *Histriomastix*), 32, 42, see "Troyeles."
tropic, 51.
"Troyeles and creasse daye," 146.
True Reporte of the Death and Martyrdom of Thomas Campion, The, 43.
True Soldiers, 120.
Tubrio, 12.

Tucca, 22, 104, 110, 113-116, 121-125, 129-133, 135.
turgidous, 117.
Tweedle, Timothy, 75.
Twelfth Night, 65, 66, 86, 151.

UDAL, NICHOLAS, 105.
Underwoods, 10, 120, 123.
un-in-one-breath-utterable skill, 26.
Untruss, Second, 46, 48, 64, 105, 114, 117, 118.

Vaughn, Sir Rees ap, 119-123; 126, 127.
venerie, Jonson given to, 2, 4, 40, 78.
ventosity, 117, 118.
Virgidemiarum, see Hall, Joseph.
VIRGIL, 104, 106.
Virgil, 109.

WARD, A., 109, 138, 145.
"War of the Theatres," the term, 1, 2; duration of the, 105; ended for Jonson, 118; allusion to, in *What You Will*, 141; plays concerned in the, 152.
Warning for Fair Women, A, 15.
WARTON, THOMAS, 48.
WATSON, THOMAS, 30.
WEBBE, WILLIAM, 93.
WELCH, CHARLES, 86.
Wellbred, 14, 17, 18, 23-27.
WESTON, HIEROME, 120.
WHALLEY, PETER, 104.
What You Will, 1, 118, 137-143, 151.
WHEATLEY, H. B., 21.
WHETSTONE, GEORGE, 14.
whippe, Ramnusia's, 35.
William Rufus, see Rufus.
Winifride, 72.
Winter's Tale, 16.
WOOD, HENRY, 34, 42, 43, 116.
WOODWARD, Henslowe servant to, 62.

York, 15, 16.
Yorkshire Tragedy, The, 77.

Zodiac, 51.

www.ingramcontent.com/pod-product-compliance
Lightning Source LLC
Chambersburg PA
CBHW020304170426
43202CB00008B/490